INTRODUCING

Chomsky

John Maher • Judy Groves

Edited by Richard Appignanesi

Icon Books UK   Totem Books USA

This edition published in the UK in 2004 by Icon Books Ltd., The Old Dairy, Brook Road, Thriplow, Royston SG8 7RG email: info@iconbooks.co.uk www.iconbooks.co.uk

This edition published in the USA in 2005 by Totem Books Inquiries to: Icon Books Ltd., The Old Dairy, Brook Road, Thriplow, Royston SG8 7RG, UK

Sold in the UK, Europe, South Africa and Asia by Faber and Faber Ltd., 3 Queen Square, London WC1N 3AU or their agents

Distributed to the trade in the USA by National Book Network Inc., 4720 Boston Way, Lanham, Maryland 20706

Distributed in the UK, Europe, South Africa and Asia by TBS Ltd., Frating Distribution Centre, Colchester Road, Frating Green, Colchester CO7 7DW

Distributed in Canada by Penguin Books Canada, 10 Alcorn Avenue, Suite 300, Toronto, Ontario M4V 3B2

This edition published in Australia in 2004 by Allen and Unwin Pty. Ltd., PO Box 8500, 83 Alexander Street, Crows Nest, NSW 2065

ISBN 1 84046 589 1

Previously published in the UK and Australia in 1996 under the title *Chomsky for Beginners* and in 1999 under the current title

Reprinted 1998, 2001, 2003

Originating editor: Richard Appignanesi

Printed and bound in Singapore by Tien Wah Press Ltd.

Introducing Chomsky

Noam Chomsky's significance as a linguist and social reformer makes him one of the 20th century's most challenging figures.

> YOU HAVE ARGUED THAT THE STRUCTURING PRINCIPLES OF HUMAN LANGUAGE ARE INNATE. THIS IS STILL A CONTROVERSIAL IDEA.

JOHN MAHER

NOAM CHOMSKY

> It is. In my view, the human brain has an innate language faculty and part of this biological endowment is a system of principles common to all languages, which is the topic of the theory of "Universal Grammar".

There are two "Chomskys". One has introduced new perspectives on language and human creativity; the other has rigorously criticized social injustice and state violence wherever these occur in the world. Both Chomskys can be seen as one and the same heir to the Enlightenment tradition. Let's begin with Chomsky the linguist.

Being and Language

Language is our humanity. Language is used to understand ourselves and others, to deal with the reality of our world and engage in acts of meaning.

The Language Bell

Language is like a bell. It sounds and it means. Sound is the external face of language. It is merely a series of disturbances in the air. The cluster or sequence of sounds,

in Japanese mean nothing in themselves. When language gongs, it comes into contact with the mind. The sound carries internal meanings which are present to the mind ("It's 6pm. Time to go home"). Thus, we see the interface between how the sound is represented, **Phonetic Form** (**PF**), and how the meaning is represented, the **Logical Form** (**LF**). **Syntax** (an intervening structure) connects the two.

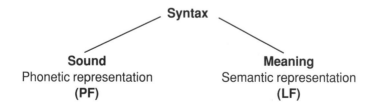

What is the nature of the bridge between sound and meaning, and how does a child manage to acquire the syntactic interface?

5

Language Use

Language is textually complex, ranging from thousands of floating "uh, huh" **conversational fillers** to massive **narratives** which encode philosophical thoughts and powerful emotions.

WITH ONE BRIEF SPEECH ACT, WE CAN BE LEGALLY MARRIED, LAUNCH AN OCEAN LINER OR CONDEMN A PERSON TO DEATH.

We each have a highly personal way of using language (**idiolect**) in a speech community which displays regional characteristics (**dialect**). Likewise, we are hooked up to multiple **stylistic** networks.

THE *GENDERLECTS* OF MAN AND WOMAN.

THE *SOCIOLECTS* OF DOCTOR AND SPORTS COMMENTATOR.

The changing language of the "I" as it journeys from infancy to old age.

How Do We Know Language?

Speakers of languages constantly cross paths, **borrowing** and **switching**. Sometimes new types of makeshift mixed languages occur, like **pidgins**, which when stabilized, become **creoles**. Through their channels of speech, writing and sign (deaf-sign), languages traverse great distances throughout time and space.

THEY CAN ENDURE PHYSICAL EXTREMES: INUIT LANGUAGES IN THE COLD NIGHTS OF THE ARCTIC TUNDRA.

ILLONGO IN THE HEAT OF THE VISAYAN ISLANDS IN THE PHILIPPINES.

THERE ARE SOME 5000 MEMBERS IN THE COMPANY OF LANGUAGES WITHIN THE BORDERS OF LESS THAN 200 NATIONS.

All these phenomena share in the form of life known as "language".

What constitutes our **knowledge** of language? In order to answer this question, we must take several strides back from what is apparently "present to the mind".

7

The Diversity Diversion

Language is so close to our Being that we frequently do not notice it. Bewildered by the differences found in **language diversity** and people's ability to use a language, we pay little attention to potential similarities. For example, dialects A and B may be superficially remote – the speakers may be almost unintelligible to each other.

A. West Yorkshire English

AH WERE REET CHUFFED ME. IT WERE SILING DAAN BUT AH KEPT LAKIN IN T' GINNEL ANYROAD.

B. Standard British

I WAS VERY PLEASED. IT WAS RAINING HEAVILY BUT I KEPT PLAYING IN THE ALLEY ANYHOW.

These speakers in fact share a central core of common rules and processes. They both "know" the same language.

Getting to the Core of Language

The underlying structures of language may be invariant sleepers over long historical eras. The common core of the language very rarely changes.

BUT WHAT STANDPOINT OUGHT WE TO ADOPT TO FIND OUT WHAT CONSTITUTES A PERSON'S KNOWLEDGE OF A LANGUAGE?

ONLY WITH THE PROPER "PSYCHIC DISTANCE" DO WE NOTICE THAT THE SIMILARITIES ARE *MARKED* AND THE DIVERGENCES *MARGINAL*.

LANGUAGE, LIKE THE MOVEMENT OF THE PLANETS AND GRAVITATIONAL CONSTANTS, IS TAKEN FOR GRANTED. PEOPLE HAVE NO INTUITION ABOUT THE RULES OF CLASSICAL PHYSICS.

Perhaps literature will forever give far deeper insight into "the full human person" than any model of scientific inquiry can hope to do. *Chomsky*

How Do We Explain Language?

Too often we prefer transparent explanation, near to the surface. The classical philosophy of the mind – both **rationalist** and **empiricist** – is deeply flawed in its assumption that the content of the mind is accessible to introspection.

THE ASPECTS OF THINGS THAT ARE MOST IMPORTANT TO US ARE HIDDEN BECAUSE OF THEIR FAMILIARITY (ONE IS UNABLE TO NOTICE SOMETHING BECAUSE IT IS ALWAYS BEFORE ONE'S EYES).

LUDWIG WITTGENSTEIN

Analysis of language is not straightforward. It is by no means transparent, least of all its definition.

DO WE NOT SHARE LANGUAGE WITH OTHER ANIMALS WHO COMMUNICATE AND THEREBY POSSESS LANGUAGE? DOLPHIN? CHIMPANZEE? WHALE? DANCING *BEE?*

Language and Communication

Chomsky asserts that language is unique to the human species, and a common part of our shared **biological endowment**. But what does "biological endowment" mean? What does a "species property" imply?

To say that language is a **biological attribute** is to say that some of its deepest properties are genetically determined, like many other aspects of who and what we are.

SO IT'S POINTLESS TO EXPECT ANIMALS TO SPEAK?

CORRECT. PIGS CAN'T FLY AND DOLPHINS CAN'T SPEAK.

But isn't language "communication" – or more precisely an instrument of communication?

Two Common Uses of Language

1. Social relations

Perhaps the statistically most common use is simply to construct and strengthen social relations among individuals.

2. Self-expression

CASUAL CONVERSATION IS PROBABLY MOTIVATED BY THE NEED TO CREATE SOCIAL BONDS WITHIN A COMFORTABLE SOCIAL MATRIX.

IN MUCH, PERHAPS MOST CONVERSATION, ONE HAS NO NEED OF "INSTRUMENTAL ENDS".

LANGUAGE CAN BE USED, AND COMMONLY IS USED, SIMPLY FOR SELF-EXPRESSION OR FOR CLARIFYING ONE'S THOUGHT.

Whilst animals employ some types of communication systems, there is nothing in animal communication which approximates to the distinctive features of human language, such as how the relationships between words are organized, namely language's **structure dependence**.

Another important example is the **discrete infinity** of natural language. There's no longest sentence (infinity), and no six-and-a-half word sentence in addition to six- and seven-word sentences, etc. (discreteness). That property is unknown in the animal world.

12

Structure Dependence

Another important defining characteristic of language is **structure dependence**. This is a universal principle common to the syntax of all languages. Knowing a language is to know not a mere string or **linear sequence** of words but their **structural relationship**. The child unerringly uses **computationally complex** rules involving structure dependence to distinguish between: "Is the girl who has freckles Rosie?" and "Has the girl who freckles is Rosie?"

Structure dependence is involved when elements of a sentence are moved to form questions or passives or reflexives. Here are two examples.

The principle is not a structural feature of one particular language, but applies to them all.

The Knowledge of Language

Chomsky's essential purpose is to ask questions about how speakers of a language organize their **knowledge**, so that a form is this way and not that way, or that a syntactical structure is like this or that.

A baby starts from an **initial zero state** or **S** with no knowledge of language, and journeys through a sequence of stages $S^1, S^2, S^3 \ldots$ navigating a sky-high mass of data and finally arriving at a **steady state** or **S'**. From then on, state change is marginal.

Thinking about the mass of language and also what is going on in the mind-brain of the child, Chomsky introduces a useful distinction:

E-language and **I-language**.

E-Language and I-Language

Chomsky originally developed the notion of **competence**, whi
system of knowledge that a native speaker possesses. This cognitive
system or domain is reformulated, rather differently, as **I-language**: a
state of the mind-brain. I-language is what a child acquires when it learns
language: an instantiation of the initial state. It is highly abstract, remote
from ordinary behaviour and mechanisms. By contrast, **E-language**
means external, extensional, any concept of language that is not internal
to the mind-brain. So, if one refers to "Irish" as the language they talk
where it is dotted orange on a map of Ireland, that's a case of E-language.
It bears conceptual resemblance but no special relation to the earlier
term **performance** – how language is actually used. E-language relates
neither to competence nor performance, which are about organisms, nor
to complicated socio-political constructs.

YOUR DISTINCTION
BETWEEN *I*-LANGUAGE
AND *E*-LANGUAGE IS
QUITE CHALLENGING.

The reason for it is simple.
Because E-language is
intended to be incoherent,
so there is no way to
understand it.

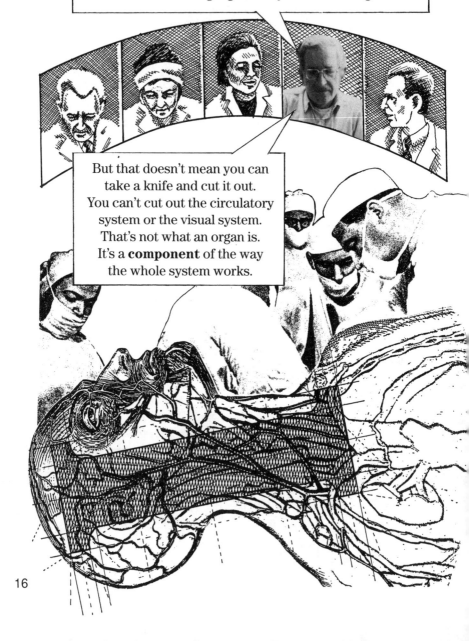

I-language is instead a very simple notion. We start with an empirical assumption which seems plausible. There is some part of the mind-brain dedicated specifically to language. Just as there is a part dedicated to vision, so there is a language faculty. It's like an organ.

But that doesn't mean you can take a knife and cut it out. You can't cut out the circulatory system or the visual system. That's not what an organ is. It's a **component** of the way the whole system works.

Systems have special function components. One assumption is that the language faculty is one such component. It has an initial state – we know that the state **changes**. What I do is different from what you do. Not too much different, so that we can loosely say we're speaking the same language.

TO A MARTIAN WE PROBABLY LOOK ALIKE.

There's no answer to whether we look alike. There's no answer to whether we speak the same language.

There are apparently wide differences, but they all come from the same initial state.

The system goes through initial states and appears to stabilize at several varying points, around the age of six and around puberty. Like other biological systems, language matures and changes, the environment affects it, although rather marginally in fact. To have an I-language **L** is to have a language faculty in a certain state. My visual system is different (state **S**) from yours (state **S'**), because of early childhood experience etc., but close enough so that we can see things in the same way for ordinary purposes. It is the same with language. Mine is in state **L**, yours is in state **L'**, close enough for us to interact.

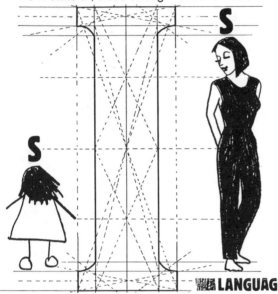
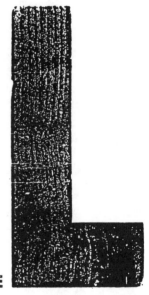

LANGUAGE

But the word "I" is there to warn that it's a technical notion.

"I" makes use of a convenient accident of English. This is an approach to language which is **individual**. It's **internalist**, like every other mode of biology. It's **intentional** in the sense of describing a function of intention.

So that's I-language. It's a technical notion. It's as close as you can get to the intuitive notion of language – the theoretical study of language.

WHAT ABOUT *E*-LANGUAGE?

Well, E-language is just **everything else**. Any other concept of language that anyone can invent. It's external. It's not inside you. It's an "other" kind of phenomenon. Possibly, there's no coherent notion of E-language. But there are people who disagree.

CAN YOU GIVE US SOME EXAMPLES?

Grammar or Politics?

There's a view that a language is a set of grammatical expressions. That makes no sense at all, yet it's a very common view.

Another view is that language is some kind of socio-political phenomenon. It's like the notion "region". The world isn't divided into regions, but we use the notion all the time because it's useful.

Similarly, the world is not divided into languages, which is not to say that we shouldn't use the notion "Chinese". Chinese is no more a language than Romance, but it serves as a map. There is no problem about the concept "Chinese", just as it is okay to say that I live in the Boston area, as long as no one is confused enough to think that the world is divided into objective areas. Italian used to be a second language for many people on the Italian Peninsula, but now it's a first language. Now that **means** something. But there's no theory of this.

American Structuralism

Chomsky takes the view that the true purpose of linguistics is not a cartography of language. It is more than a voyage through a chaotic mass of E-language (however interesting it is to map such a thing). Much of linguistic inquiry has been dedicated to that approach. American structuralism was founded upon the empirical tradition, and set itself the task of giving an organized account of masses of linguistic data.

Leonard Bloomfield (1887–1949), the pre-eminent figure of American linguistics, stressed that . . .

> ONLY DIRECT OBSERVATION OF LINGUISTIC EVENTS CAN YIELD STATEMENTS ABOUT LANGUAGE.

Chomsky declared his conceptual break with the empiricist tradition. In his epoch-making work, *Syntactic Structures* (1957), Chomsky nailed his manifesto to the door.

> A theory is not a taxonomy, an organization of lots of data. It is a rigorous description of a "possible human language".

To this end, the central question accordingly must be: what kind of grammatical processes are possible and which are impossible. 21

What About Saussure?

> **FERDINAND DE SAUSSURE** (1857-1913) IS WIDELY REGARDED AS HAVING HAD ENORMOUS IMPACT ON THE FIELD OF LINGUISTICS. WHAT DO YOU THINK ARE THE BASIC CONTRIBUTIONS AND FLAWS OF HIS LINGUISTICS?

Well, one flaw is that it is so limited in what it covers. I don't think Saussure himself took it all that seriously, to tell you the truth. He had to teach a course in General Linguistics. But he didn't say much. I've been through the notebooks, which are more interesting than the published part. It's okay. But really there's nothing much there. If you wanted to **teach** it, you wouldn't really know what to teach.

FERDINAND DE SAUSSURE

Contributions? I frankly don't think the field would be all that different if it hadn't existed. It made people focus their attention on the fact of **structures** and not just listings of items. American structuralism had similar ideas coming from a different source. It was going to happen.

The sequence from Saussure to the Prague School* of Roman Jakobson and others certainly had a positive effect. Now it's just absorbed into a way of looking at things. On the semantics side, it's doubtful that there was much of an influence. On the general conceptual side, I think it's mostly confusing. I don't know what **langue** is. It's certainly not structure.

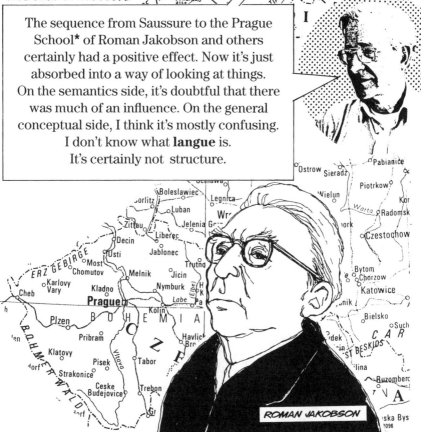

ROMAN JAKOBSON

*In the late 1920s and early 30s the Prague School formulated a theory of **phonology** in which sounds are analyzed in sets of distinctive oppositions.

23

WHO WOULD YOU COMMEND AS A MORE SIGNIFICANT FIGURE IN LINGUISTICS?

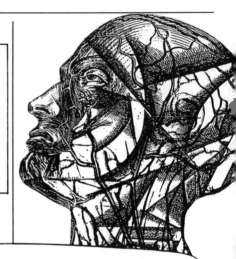

Certainly, Jespersen at about the same time had a more serious conception. He is at the end of a long tradition in his formulation of the notion that there is an innate structure in the mind. It underlies free expressions and linguistic use as an individual property.

I ARGUED THAT IT IS LIKELY TO INVOLVE *MORPHOLOGY* AND THE *LEXICON.*

That's right, because if anything is going to vary in language, it would be at the morphological end.

Otto Jespersen (1860–1943) was a Danish linguist and an authority on English grammar and language teaching. Jespersen pioneered a movement to base foreign language teaching on everyday speech. He published his influential *Growth and Structure of the English Language* in 1905, and the seven-volume *Modern English Grammar* (1909–49).

I EXPLORED THE RELATION BETWEEN SOUND AND SENSE IN LANGUAGE AND WAS MUCH INFLUENCED BY DARWIN'S EVOLUTIONARY THEORIES.

Among his most important achievements was the delineation of a "logic" of grammar in which he would reject key tenets of Saussurian linguistics, anticipating modern theories of syntax and child language acquisition.

25

Galileo's Method

How then do you analyze language?

I adopt a **Galilean style** of inquiry applied to language. The main features of this method involve **Abstraction** and **Idealization**.

WHAT WAS GALILEO'S METHOD?

IN REVERSING ARISTOTLE'S THEORY OF THE EARTH-CENTRED UNIVERSE, I HAD TO NARROW MY IDEA OF MOTION JUST TO MECHANICAL MOTION. I HAD TO THROW OVERBOARD A LOT OF OTHER POSSIBLY HELPFUL THEORIES, AND LIVE WITH THE FACT THAT IN MY THEORY THERE WERE THINGS I COULD NOT EXPLAIN.

Galileo Galilei (1564–1642), Italian astronomer, supported the Copernican theory of the solar system. In his experiments with falling objects and the pendulum, he advanced the principles of observation in science.

Chomsky is interested in the question: to what extent and in what ways can inquiry in the "Galilean style" yield understanding of the roots of human nature in the **cognitive** domain?

Can we hope to move beyond superficiality by a readiness to undertake perhaps far-reaching idealization and to construct abstract models that are accorded more significance than the ordinary world of sensation, and correspondingly, by readiness to tolerate unexplained phenomena or even as yet unexplained counter-evidence to theoretical constructions that have achieved a certain degree of explanatory adequacy in some limited domain? *Chomsky, Rules and Representation*

Abstraction

In the Galilean method, an abstract model is constructed which yields a higher degree of reality than can be obtained by depending on the world of sensations. But in far-reaching abstraction we move beyond the ordinary world of language.

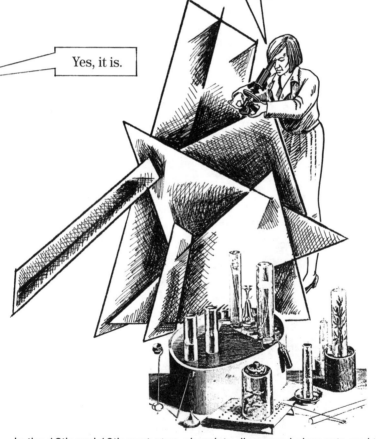

In the 18th and 19th centuries, chemists discussed elements and their properties, the Periodic Table, valence, Benzene and the like. These were **abstract** entities to be related ultimately to **physical** entities, then unknown, that would exhibit the properties formulated at an abstract level

of description.

"Language is a method of conveying our ideas to the minds of other persons: and the grammar of any language is a collection of observations on the structure of it, and a system of rules for the proper use of it."
Preface To The Rudiments of English Grammar (1772).
Joseph Priestley (1733–1804), scientist and grammarian.

Idealization

Chomsky is an **ideal-type** linguist.

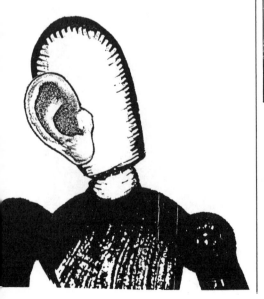

For the sake of theoretical explanation, I do two things. I devise the notion of the **ideal speaker-hearer** and leave out the time factor in language acquisition.

Consider the latter step. Chomsky hypothesizes that the mechanism known as **Universal Grammar** constructs an **instantaneous** grammar of the language. This is based upon the assumption that nothing in the actual progress of language-acquisition would affect the process, making the result different from a situation in which the language was acquired in an instant.

Ideal-Type

Ideal-type is a term invented by **Max Weber** (1864–1920), a German philosopher and socio-political theorist. It is typical of social science methodology which starts from the view that not all judgements should be of empirical fact.

ECONOMIC THEORY MAKES CERTAIN ASSUMPTIONS WHICH SCARCELY EVER CORRESPOND COMPLETELY WITH REALITY, BUT WHICH APPROXIMATE IT IN VARIOUS DEGREES, AND ASKS: "HOW WOULD MEN ACT UNDER THESE ASSUMED CONDITIONS, IF THEIR ACTIONS WERE ENTIRELY RATIONAL?"

ECONOMY AND SOCIETY

Weber stressed the need for objectivity in examining the relationships between ideology, religions, social structure and material value.

And there is abstraction in political economy too. Consider how abstraction operates in Marx's theory of capital.

INDIVIDUALS ARE DEALT WITH ONLY IN SO FAR AS THEY ARE THE PERSONIFICATIONS OF ECONOMIC CATEGORIES, EMBODIMENTS OF PARTICULAR CLASS-RELATIONS AND CLASS INTERESTS.

The speakers of a language typically do not understand the theory of their language, just as people typically do not understand the theory of their visual system. In both cases, the theory is an idealization, omitting many factors considered to be irrelevant to the purpose at hand, and seeking to discover deeper principles that these factors obscure.

Violating the Rose

FAR-OFF, MOST SECRET AND INVIOLATE ROSE,
ENFOLD ME . . .
W.B.YEATS, "THE SECRET ROSE"

Rational inquiry into the nature of all physical and mental reality, including language, proceeds by means of extracting away from **variation**. Consider a rose, for instance. We can describe its shape and colour and lovely fragrance.

But once we start to describe it as "an organism" – our standpoint regarding the pulse and flow of nutrients or the oxygen-carbon dioxide cycle – the rose in all its apparent beauty seems to disappear in the flux of chemical processes.

In fact, we have only bracketed the fragrance, not denied its reality. It is simply that our purpose and standpoint have changed. Now, what is true of Marxian theory and the rose is true of language.

33

The Idealized Model

Linguistic theory is concerned primarily with an **ideal speaker-listener** in a completely homogeneous speech community who knows its language perfectly and is unaffected by such grammatically irrelevant conditions as . . .

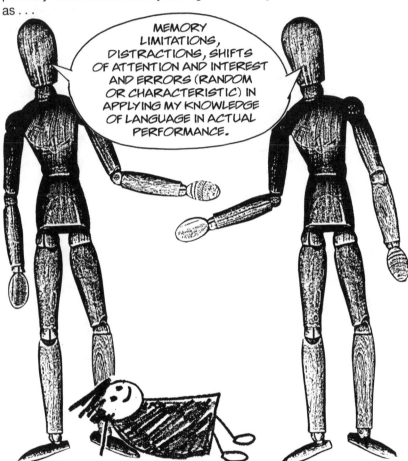

MEMORY LIMITATIONS, DISTRACTIONS, SHIFTS OF ATTENTION AND INTEREST AND ERRORS (RANDOM OR CHARACTERISTIC) IN APPLYING MY KNOWLEDGE OF LANGUAGE IN ACTUAL PERFORMANCE.

We thus make a fundamental distinction between **competence** (the speaker-hearer's knowledge of this language) and **performance** (the actual use of language in concrete situations). Only under idealized conditions is performance a **direct reflection** of competence. A record of natural speech will show numerous false starts, deviations from rules, changes of plan in mid-course and so on. The problem for the linguist, as well as for the child learning the language, is to determine, from the data of performance, the underlying system of rules that has been mastered by the speaker-hearer and that he puts to use in actual performance.

A grammar of a language purports to be a description of the ideal speaker-hearer's intrinsic competence.
Chomsky

In order to make language an object of rational inquiry, we consider diversity and variation as irrelevant to this stage of investigation. Let us construct an idealization: a community of speakers in which no stylistic or dialectal or variation of any other sort exists.

IMPOSSIBLE IN THE REAL WORLD OF LANGUAGE. IT CAN'T WORK. IT IS NOT A TRUE REPRESENTATION OF LANGUAGE.

Yes, but in this ideal, homogeneous imagined speech community, knowledge of the language is uniformly represented in the mind of each person. By means of a far-reaching abstraction which postulates such uniformity, we can then term each community member an **ideal speaker-hearer**.

35

Language as a Mental Organ

We can study the problem of language *and mind* in much the same Galilean way as we study any problem of biology. To study the human visual system, we would first attempt to abstract it from its physical context – its interaction with the circulatory and many other systems. By the process of idealization, the scientist tries to discover the structural principles that determine how the system functions – how the system develops in the organism from the initial genetic codes to its mature state.

When we view language as a **cognitive** – that is, a **mental organ** as an analogue to a physical one – we ask the very same questions. What are the structural principles by which this mental organ functions? What are the functions of the system?

BUT DOES NOT THE NOTION OF A "MENTAL ORGAN" FLY HEAD- ON INTO THE "MIND-BODY PROBLEM"?

Descartes' Theory of Body

There is no problem of **mind-body**. The mind-body problem could only arise and be formulated because of a notion of "body" defined in terms of **Cartesian mechanics** – a kind of contact mechanics dealing with pushing and pulling and colliding – proposed by **René Descartes** (1596–1650), the French philosopher and mathematician.

ALL THE PHENOMENA OF THE WORLD OF INANIMATE OBJECTS, ANIMALS AND THE FUNCTIONING OF THE HUMAN BODY CAN BE EXPLAINED IN TERMS OF THE BEHAVIOUR OF A *MACHINE*, DETERMINED BY THE BEHAVIOUR OF ITS PARTS AND THE EXTERNAL ENVIRONMENT.

But human language does not fall within this domain. Ordinary human discourse is unbounded, innovative, independent of stimulus or control, but at the same time coherent and situationally appropriate – what I would call "the creative aspect of language use".

37

The Cartesians sought richer principles to account for phenomena which exceeded the limits of Cartesian mechanics, and thus they posited a second substance, a *res cogitans* – a "thinking substance" distinct and separate from body and interacting with it in a way that was the topic of much inquiry and controversy.

THIS THINKING SUBSTANCE IS WHAT WE CALL "MIND".

The long-running drama called **The Mind-Body Problem** has been entirely mis-staged in the theatre of philosophy instead of the theatre of science. The proper title of the piece should be "Brain and Mind".

Talk about the mind is talk about the brain at a certain level. Just as talk about the orbits of the planets is talk about physical entities at a certain level.

Classical formulations of the mind-body problem were conducted by people whom we call philosophers – Descartes and Leibniz, for example – but who regarded themselves as what we now call "scientists".

Our current distinction between science and philosophy did not even exist in the period of these classical inquiries.

Even the empiricist **David Hume** (1711–76) referred to his work in terms of a scientific and specifically cognitive enterprise, defining his moral philosophy as "the science of human nature". This was a branch of the sciences concerned with "the secret springs and principles by which the human mind is actuated in its operations", essentially innate ideas, in the Cartesian sense.

I REGARDED MY ENTERPRISE AS ANALOGOUS TO THE PHYSICAL INQUIRIES OF ISAAC NEWTON.

39

A New Theory of Body

The Cartesian theory of body quickly collapsed under the weight of Newtonian discoveries. We now no longer have a definite concept of the body. Rather, the **theory of body** – or physics – is formulated in concepts of forces, waves, particles, etc.

We can no longer ask whether some phenomenon falls outside the range of "body". We can only ask whether our current concepts of "body" are adequate to account for some phenomena.

IF NOT, YOU MUST EXTEND AND MODIFY YOUR BASIC PHYSICS, JUST AS I EXTENDED CARTESIAN MECHANICS TO ACCOUNT FOR THE MOTION OF THE HEAVENLY BODIES.

NEWTON

The problem now is twofold. To investigate the phenomena of the mind, and to seek to relate them to the natural sciences by discovering the physical mechanisms that exhibit the properties and principles that we find in our inquiry into the mind.

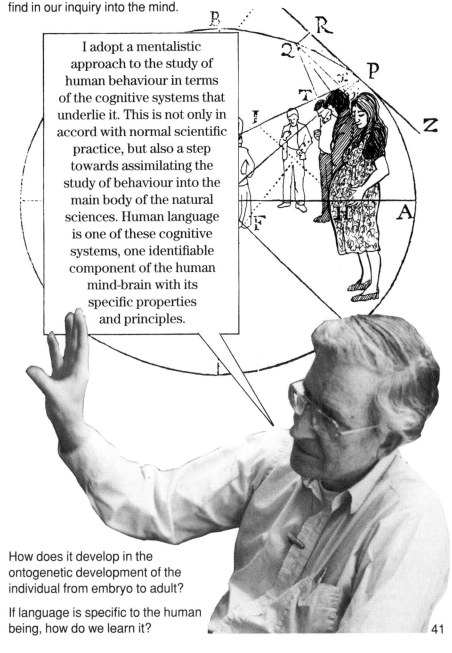

I adopt a mentalistic approach to the study of human behaviour in terms of the cognitive systems that underlie it. This is not only in accord with normal scientific practice, but also a step towards assimilating the study of behaviour into the main body of the natural sciences. Human language is one of these cognitive systems, one identifiable component of the human mind-brain with its specific properties and principles.

How does it develop in the ontogenetic development of the individual from embryo to adult?

If language is specific to the human being, how do we learn it?

41

Skinner's Behaviourist Theory

Behavior is shaped and maintained by its consequences.
B.F. Skinner, *Beyond Freedom and Dignity*

Burrhus F. Skinner (1904–90), Professor of Psychology at Harvard University, extrapolated from stimulus-response behaviour in animals to the linguistic behaviour of humans. Behaviour is determined by the reinforcement received from the environment. Rats threading their way through a maze trigger a spring, accidentally reproducing the behaviour that Skinner wants to reinforce. He then rewards them with food pellets.

"We can also reinforce someone by emitting verbal behavior, . . . by not emitting verbal behavior (keeping silent and paying attention) . . . or by acting appropriately on some future occasion . . ." B.F. Skinner

The Refutation of Behaviourism

In 1959, Chomsky composed a basic refutation of behaviourist psychology in his review of B.F. Skinner's **Verbal Behavior**. According to Chomsky, children are not born *tabula rasa*. On the contrary, each child is genetically predisposed to structure how knowledge is acquired.

The phrase "X is **reinforced** by Y" is being used as a cover term for X **wants** Y, X **likes** Y, X **wishes** Y were the case, etc. Invoking the term "reinforcement" has no explanatory force, and any idea that this paraphrase introduces any new clarity or objectivity into the description of wishing, liking, etc., is a serious delusion.

Skinner's account rejects all postulations of inner states and sees human behaviour as entirely a function of antecedent events. For Chomsky, this reduction of human behaviour to "conditioned responses" contradicts the actual complexity and freedom of consciousness.

43

To understand the difference in approach between Chomsky's **mental state theory** and Skinner's **Behaviourism**, let us imagine there are two moonships . . .

Moonship BFS 1 is designed according to an original theory of B.F. Skinner. It is manned by pigeons who look at a screen which shows exactly what's going on ahead.

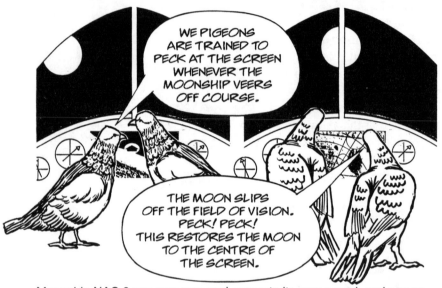

Moonship NAC 2 can measure and compute its own speed, and use an internalized theory to plot its course and make the necessary adjustments to its position.

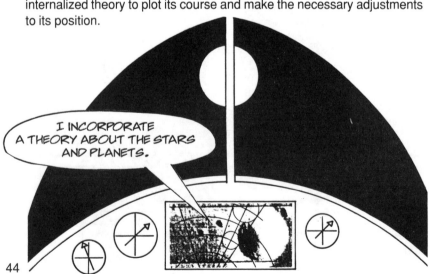

Now, of course, it is quite possible that both rockets might hit the moon, according to target. On the surface, therefore, they appear the same; but we need to look deeper.

This cognizing moonship NAC 2 shares properties with human knowledge. This difference has important consequences for the question of human freedom.

If people are, in fact, malleable **plastic beings** with no essential psychological nature, then why should they not be controlled and coerced by those who claim authority, special knowledge, and a unique insight into what is best for those less enlightened?

Plato's Problem

How is it that in our passage through the world we can know and expect and understand so much from so little? How is it that our human contact with life is so brief, personal and limited and nevertheless can yield so much? Chomsky calls this puzzle the **poverty of the stimulus**.

We may be materially and intellectually impoverished, physically sick, lack will and concentration, have lifelong borderline personality problems, and despite all this, the mind's cognitive system goes on building its edifice quietly, uniformly, seemingly beyond our control.

WE KNOW SO MUCH BECAUSE WE REMEMBER SO MUCH. REMINISCENCES OF A PRE-EXISTENCE.
PLATO

Gottfried Leibniz (1646–1716) was unhappy with this explanation, but was in tune with Plato's central observation. Following Leibniz, Chomsky can formulate the conception that the knowledge human beings possess derives from the innate qualities of mind.

MAYBE "REMINISCENCES OF A PRE-EXISTENCE" SIMPLY MEANS INNATE QUALITIES OF THE MIND?
GOTTFRIED LEIBNIZ

IF ALL WE ARE IS A "BEAST-MACHINE" THAT TALKS – THEN HOW IS IT WE CAN BE SO CREATIVE IN LANGUAGE?
DESCARTES

Language Is Not Learned, It Grows

The term "language learning" has had its day. It is a relic of the past. A child does not **learn** language. It **grows** in the mind-brain of the child.

Now, children do not receive a grammar book to sort things out for them. They do not even get the relevant experience that allows them to make inductive generalizations – for instance, that "each other" takes a plural antecedent.

CHILDREN MAKE LOTS OF ERRORS, BUT THEY DO NOT ASSUME THAT "THE MEN WANTED ME TO LISTEN TO EACH OTHER" IS A WELL-FORMED SEN- TENCE MEANING "EACH OF THE MEN WANTED ME TO LISTEN TO EACH OTHER".

Children already bring a package of relevant information to the process of **language acquisition**. With this, they can progress to more and more mature states of knowledge.

47

Innateness

Chomsky employs the term **innate**, and means by this not that language is already completed, sitting waiting in the brain of the child, ready to be spoken. Rather, the child has a genetic programme, a blueprint which comes into use when the child is ready. An infant dipping into the mind for the thing called "language" will not find an over-the-counter take-away, but rather a recipe-book of a few simple procedures and process rules.

AND THAT RECIPE-BOOK REMAINS, OF COURSE, UNAVAILABLE FOR ORDINARY VIEWING.

Language arises in the mind-brain of the child as a specific realization of the language faculty, which passes through three states:

An **initial state**

A **series of states** (as the child matures in a speech community)

A **steady state** (at or before puberty)

The steady state changes only in relatively superficial ways, mainly by acquisition of new vocabulary items that satisfy the conditions of the acquired language. Acquiring a language is less something that a child does than something that happens to the child, like growing arms rather than wings, or undergoing puberty at a certain stage of maturation. These processes depend on external events, but the basic lines of development are *internally determined*.

YOU DON'T EXPECT YOUR THUMB TO KEEP ON GROWING.

Right. And with language growth, you can see the constraints by doing a careful analysis of cognitive processes, such as linguistic processes. That's why linguistics is so important.

49

Growth and Constraints on Learning

Supporting the notion that language grows in the mind-brain, Chomsky draws upon the metaphor of **James Harris**, the 18th century philosopher.

The growth of knowledge . . . [resembles] . . . the growth of Fruit; however external causes may in some degree cooperate, it is the internal vigour, and virtue of the tree, that must ripen the juices to their maturity.

The doctrine, designed within the intellectual tradition, that human mentality is perfectly plastic and that humans can learn anything is a mistake. Human mentality is highly constrained. It can develop in some directions and not others.

Language is Not Imitation

And what about **imitation**? Few people have suggested that we undergo puberty because of peer pressure or by watching other people do it. We do not know what factors determine the onset of puberty, but we rationally take it for granted that it is an internally directed system.

SO LANGUAGE PURSUES ITS NATURAL COURSE?

WE KNOW MORE ABOUT LANGUAGE THROUGH THEORETICAL AND EMPIRICAL INQUIRY.

Language is not defined as something "learned" or "obtained" like a social product. That raises two important questions.
1. Just what is knowledge of language?
2. How is language acquired?

What is Knowledge of Language?

Well, the standard answer to this question is that "knowledge of language is an ability, a disposition".

JUST LIKE LEARNING TO RIDE A BICYCLE, WHICH CAN BE PRACTICED. THIS WAS MY VIEW.

WITTGENSTEIN

Another answer comes in the reply to the second question: "How is language acquired?"

BY CONDITIONING, HABIT-FORMATION, "GENERAL LEARNING MECHANISMS" SUCH AS INDUCTION.

SKINNER

Now both these answers are entirely mistaken.

Suppose Song Kim learns how to play the cello and then one day suffers a serious head injury in a road accident which causes her to lose entirely her instrumental ability (though her physical capacities are unaffected).

As the brain injury heals, the music returns. What was left intact?

THE COGNITIVE SYSTEM THAT UNDERPINS MY MUSICAL SKILLS?

Now you might argue that the ability was in fact not lost, but only its **exercise** disappeared. But then that gives us **two** definitions of ability, and the concepts are quite different.

The latter definition is normal usage, and the first is an invented concept which merely means knowledge. A verbal manoeuvre. We must conclude that what was retained was a **system of knowledge**, a cognitive system of the mind-brain. Possession of this knowledge is not the same as the actual skill involved in playing Bach. In fact, Song Kim can add Bartok and improve her skills considerably with no change in knowledge.

Here's another example. Look at the way in which we form questions in English.

Patsy Rabbit ate Farmer Giles' carrot.

Now, in order to make a question you extract some phrase from the sentence, insert an interrogative word and move it to the front: What did Patsy Rabbit eat?

And the sentence:
I believe Farmer Giles saw Patsy Rabbit stealing his carrots.

You can turn this into:
What do I believe Farmer Giles saw?

But you cannot do that in every case. Like this one.
From: *I believe Farmer Giles' assertion that Patsy Rabbit was eating carrots . . .* you can't get: *What do I believe Farmer Giles' assertion that Patsy Rabbit was eating?**

Now how do I know that it's not a sentence? Was I corrected in school? Did I hear it? I don't think so, and besides, nobody makes that kind of error anyway, so I couldn't have been corrected.

**Not grammatical.*

Non-Inductive Ability

There is nothing in the environment that will tell me that the string of words in * is not grammatical. Now, if we follow a perfectly inductive procedure we would have to say that it is a proper sentence. But here we seem to be chucking out the inductive method. So what's going on? Something is alerting us to the fact that sentence * is not grammatical, and the relation between our judgement of what is or is not okay is *not an inductive one*. Any natural scientist worth his carrots must conclude that the distinction is rooted (get it?) in the nature of the organism itself.

Language learning is not something you do.
It **happens** to you.

To paraphrase John Lennon . . .

LANGUAGE IS WHAT HAPPENS WHEN YOU'RE BUSY MAKING OTHER PLANS.

"Motherese"

Of course, the environment plays its part. As a child you are placed in a social environment. What place you find yourself in determines the way in which the parameters of universal grammar are set, like whether your language is going to be Thai or Welsh. You may have a rich and stimulating environment or an impoverished one.

BUT WHAT ABOUT *MOTHERESE*, THE SIMPLIFIED LANGUAGE SPOKEN TO CHILDREN? DOESN'T THAT ALSO PLAY A PART, SINCE MOTHERESE IS CAREFULLY CONSTRUCTED? NOT ONLY THAT, THE CHILD WILL CHANGE MANY OF THE STRUCTURES AS IT GROWS UP!

Look. Motherese is not Martian language. It's different alright; but the properties that the child acquires are not significantly different. Motherese is a pretty **culture-bound** thing.

Other than in highly verbal middle-class families, most children learn to talk without anyone paying much attention to them, sometimes in the worst possible conditions.

A KID WHO LEARNS PORTUGUESE ON THE STREETS OF RIO IN BRAZIL DOESN'T HAVE THE BENEFIT OF A CAREFULLY PROGRAMMED LEARNING SYSTEM AT HIS DISPOSAL.

So the capacity to speak is the result of a mature state of mind and the interaction of two factors: the innate properties of the mind and the environment.

But remember, you find the **deep properties** of that mature state by looking at what people know about language – WHICH DOES NOT APPEAR IN THE ENVIRONMENT AT ALL. What is really interesting is **the errors that children do not make**.

"LANGUAGE IS AWAKENED IN THE MIND: ONE CAN ONLY PROVIDE THE THREAD ALONG WHICH IT WILL DEVELOP OF ITSELF."

WILHELM VON HUMBOLDT (1767-1835)
REASONS OF STATE

The Attack From the Social

Placing the environment as marginal in the growth of language provokes a chorus of critics from various quarters. The attack centres on the notion that language is primarily a social or cultural fact. The attacks come from five sources.

1. Anthropological Linguistics: as articulated in the American descriptive-linguistics tradition, represented by **Edward Sapir** (1884–1939):

WALKING IS AN INHERENT, BIOLOGICAL FUNCTION OF MAN. NOT SO LANGUAGE. SPEECH IS A NON-INSTINCTIVE, ACQUIRED CULTURAL FUNCTION.

2. Sociology: the view that the "habitus" of a social group – its socially constituted system of motivating structures or dispositions – gives rise to practices which in turn reproduce habitus.

LINGUISTIC KNOWLEDGE DERIVES FROM *LANGUAGE PRACTICE*.

3. **Political Economy**.

LANGUAGE (THE OBJECT) TAKES ITS MEANING FROM THE VARIOUS ACTIVITIES IN WHICH IT PARTICIPATES IN PARTICULAR ECONOMIC RELATIONS.

4. **Philosophy**.

SPEAKING IS PART OF A *LANGUAGE GAME* IN WHICH THE MEANING OF WORDS IS PRECISELY WHAT IT IS BY VIRTUE OF USES IN ACTUAL CONTEXTS.

5. **Humanistic**.

REDUCING LANGUAGE DEVELOPMENT TO THE MERE REFINEMENT OF A "DEVICE" IN THE BRAIN IS AN EXTREMELY MECHANISTIC AND ANTI-REALISTIC APPROACH TO THE CHILD. IN THE PROCESS, A LOT OF REAL LIFE GETS LOST.

The Reply

The so-called humanistic objection is an exquisite example of anti-intellectualism. Once you begin to abstract from a system in order to study it, you are accused of being a kind of anti-humanistic, philosophical vivisectionist. We have to look for explanatory theories to understand the world, and abstract systems are a perfectly proper way to proceed.

SO YOU ARE NOT ENTIRELY EXCLUDING THE EFFECT OF THE ENVIRONMENT?

The language faculty develops in the individual along an intrinsically determined course under the triggering effect of appropriate social interaction, and partially shaped by the environment – English is not Japanese – just as the distribution of horizontal and vertical receptors in the visual cortex can be modified by early visual experience. *Chomsky*

61

The knowledge of language a speaker has acquired constitutes an implicit theory of the language that he has mastered, a theory that predicts the grammatical structure of an infinite class of potential physical events, and the conditions for the appropriate use of each of these items. *Chomsky*

This is later expanded to a wider view of competence.

Pragmatic competence involves **knowledge of conditions and manner of appropriate use, in conformity with various purpose**.

One may therefore postulate the notion that the use of language is also governed by a system of **abstract principles**.

LANGUAGE IS SO RICH AND COMPLEX. IT CONTAINS MYRIAD STRUCTURES SO FAR BEYOND WHAT YOU CAN PICK UP IN THE ENVIRONMENT THAT UNLESS THERE IS SOME INNATE, PREDETERMINED INTELLECTUAL CAPACITY, CHILDREN WOULD NEVER LEARN LANGUAGE.

Language has infinite scope. Although it has only finite means – sounds, marks on the page, manual signs – its sentences go on and on. So surely lurking inside, at the very core of language, there must be some kind of recursive **rule system** which allows language to generate an infinite range of structures, even more than we can imagine or think we are capable of, which we can somehow produce as the beat goes on. Language itself is changing day to day and we are being confronted by new and unknown combinations of language.

So What is Linguistics?

Rationalist philosophers referred to language as a "mirror of the mind", reflecting the essential properties of the mind. The field known as linguistics is heir to that tradition. Linguistics is part of cognitive psychology, ultimately human biology. More specifically, the language faculty allows various possible realizations, i.e. specific human languages. Thus, French is one of its possible manifestations, Russian another.

Employing the notion of the ideal speaker-hearer helps us clarify what we mean by "grammar".

THE LINGUIST IS LIKE THE PHYSICIST WHO THEORIZES HOW THE SUN'S HEAT GETS TURNED INTO LIGHT. YOU CANNOT ACTUALLY GO THERE IN AN OBSERVATION PROBE. INSTEAD YOU MAKE A GOOD GUESS BY STUDYING LIGHT AT THE SUN'S OUTERMOST LAYER. SIMILARLY, A LINGUIST DESCRIBES GRAMMAR *IN THE BRAIN.*

The linguist's concern with the language faculty is with the attribute that **all** persons possess – not with variant knowledge of say Quechua or Nivkhi or Spanish. Just as what different head-shapes people possess (square, round, oblong etc.) is of no relevance in this respect. The crucial matter is that they **all** have heads.

Creative vs. Recursive

Look at this twofold character of all languages: **creative** and **recursive**. The grammatical system is recursive. We make up new sentences freely. The language generated is infinite, whilst the grammar itself is finite.

So, the rules of grammar **iterate** (Sanskrit *itara*, "the other"). Intricately cut and crafted to accommodate their *alter ego*, language, the rules of grammar generate a massive number of sentences. The grammatical system sits hard and fast as rocks on top of the waterfall, giving shape and order to the rapid torrent of water. We know how to use language in the proper situations, and we can create and grasp new sentences on new occasions.

THE BEHAVIOURIST MIGHT SAY: "SO IT'S DETERMINED BY THE ENVIRONMENT!"

No. I said that language use is "appropriate" to situations, not "controlled by a stimulus".

So, language is there available to us, utterly generous, unbounded in scope, an instrument for the free expression of thought. That is what is meant by the "**creative aspect of language use**".

The Tale of Two Grammars

The **representation** of the knowledge of these ideal speaker-hearers is what we call the "grammar" of the language.

SO THAT MEANS WE ARE REALLY TALKING ABOUT *TWO* GRAMMARS?

Yes. Grammar (1): **I-language**. Grammar (2): **theory of I-language**.

"Grammar" (1), in the sense of a structure postulated in the mind, means I-language, and (2) a theory of I-language, composed by a linguist (in the same sense in which a theory of the visual system is about the visual system).

LIKE THIS SPANISH GRAMMAR BOOK SITTING ON MY DESK?

No, the traditional grammar on your desk is a theory about some highly complex notion of E-language; fine for its purpose (Spanish), but not good for an inquiry into language beyond the basic steps.

Grammar and gas. Remember Joseph Priestley's remark? You can't open up the mind-brain and look at "grammar", but you can work with it like a scientist works with atoms and molecules. You can make a **model** of Swahili by making a complete grammar of the language. This grammar is nothing less than a full set of operational procedures. A complete grammar is a set of rules, and these rules generate the language.

We don't say that the model duplicates the actual encoding procedures of the central nervous system. However, you can get a clearer picture of the operations which generate language by developing theories of I-language (= grammar 2) that generate expressions with their structures, that is, by developing grammars (2) of these I-languages; grammar (2) being a theory of I-language (grammar 1).

So grammar (1) is somehow built into a person's nervous system. Let us look more closely at this notion.

Traditional Grammar vs. Generative Grammar

Chomsky's first major attempt to respond to the classificatory model of descriptive linguistics was **Generative Grammar**.

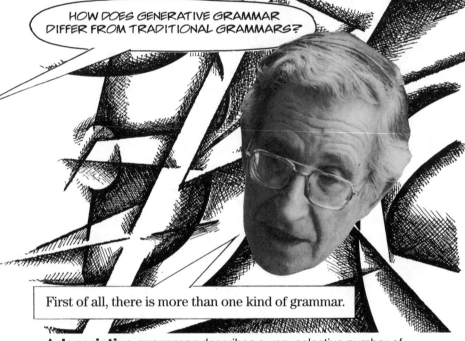

HOW DOES GENERATIVE GRAMMAR DIFFER FROM TRADITIONAL GRAMMARS?

First of all, there is more than one kind of grammar.

A **descriptive grammar** describes a very selective number of grammatical constructions that are used in a language.

A **prescriptive grammar** represents a kind of manual of attitudes to grammatical usage: good French and bad French.

A **reference grammar** is a description of as many grammatical aspects of the language as are thought useful for some particular purpose. It is meant to be an authoritative compilation of facts.

A **pedagogical grammar** is a book for teaching and learning a language.

All these grammars presuppose that the speaker knows the language, or at least has an intact and functioning language faculty. The presupposition was tacit; traditional, modern and pedagogic grammarians mistakenly thought they were describing the language. They were, at best, giving hints; good enough for a person who had the knowledge they were presupposing.

Generative grammar is a theory about a system of knowledge.

A generative grammar tries to answer the questions presupposed by all other kinds of grammar: i.e. what do speakers know that enables them to make intelligent use of the hints and examples given in standard grammars?

It is therefore a **theoretical** grammar. It attempts to answer a question: What is this system of knowledge incorporated in the mind-brain of a person who speaks and understands a particular language? What constitutes the language that the person has mastered and knows? The theory about the topic is what we call a "generative grammar".

69

Traditional grammars are a guide for people who already know something about the language. They concentrate on outlines of sentence structure, with information on irregularities, idiosyncratic facts and the like.

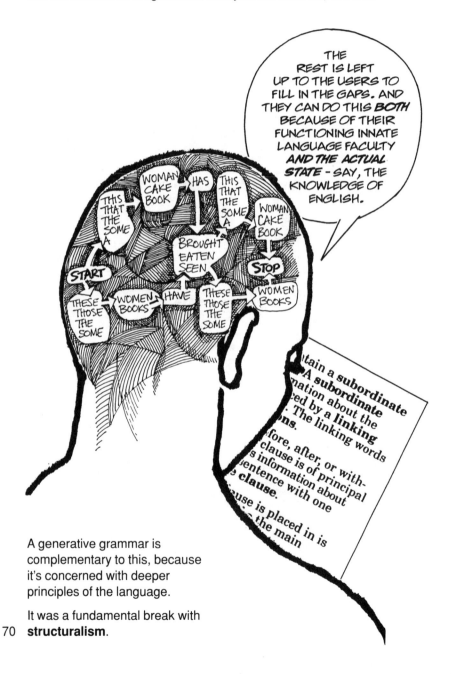

A generative grammar is complementary to this, because it's concerned with deeper principles of the language.

It was a fundamental break with **structuralism**.

The Break with Structuralism

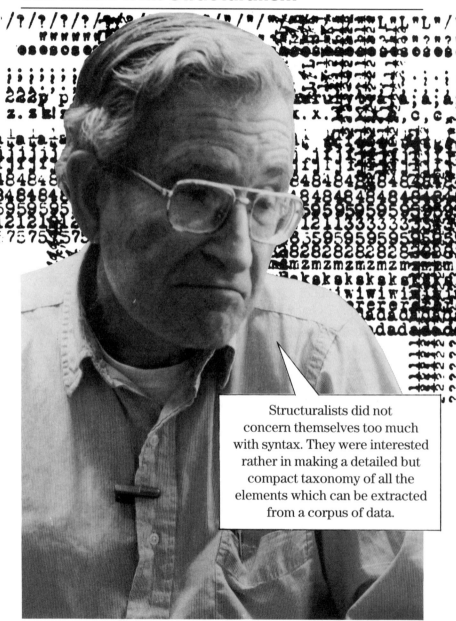

> Structuralists did not concern themselves too much with syntax. They were interested rather in making a detailed but compact taxonomy of all the elements which can be extracted from a corpus of data.

Chomsky: 1. Rejected empiricist constraints on concept formation.
2. Redefined the goal of linguistic theory towards the formal description of a "possible human language".

I'm Okay, *You're Okay But Not

We can represent a "grammar" of a language as a set of rules that specify very exactly (i.e. "generate") which sentences are **okay** ("possible sentences") and which are **not okay** (sentences like "you're okay but not" get an asterisk*) and what structural properties they possess.

SO HOW DO SYNTACTIC PROCESSES WORK?

There are two types of rules, like a pair of scissors which cut out a pattern in language in two ways.

1. Phrase Structure Rules show how a sentence is divided into its component parts (phrases). If we take the sentence, **the tailor of Leeds must be skilful**, we can write it like this . . .

S – NP / AUX / VP

the tailor of Leeds
noun phrase

must
auxiliary

be skilful
verb phrase

2. The second type of rules connect various types of sentence. For example, Murphy's Law keeps popping up in two forms. Of course, we always understand both!

Here Mrs Murphy is employing a **deletion rule** which also involves the notion that: *deleted words must have an identical counterpart which is not deleted.*

The flip side of a deletion rule is the following: Humphrey Bogart's **insertion rule**. Consider the sentence, *A storm is blowin' up*. But what does Bogart say?

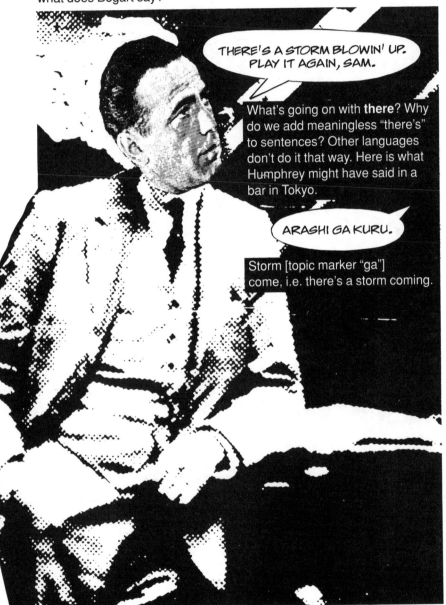

No sign of "there" there. But in the English insertion rule, you first set out
the subject of the sentence and then put in "there".

And the *there* in "there is a storm" is different from the *there* in: "Sam's piano is over there in the corner."

NOW, WE ALL KNOW THAT IF THERE'S A STORM OVERHEAD, THEN "IT'S PROBABLY RAINING".

"IT"?

Here we go again! The sentence "it's raining" is a **surface** form – what is spoken. Unlike Japanese or Tagalog and other languages, it's a strict rule that every sentence in English must employ the subject – except for specific kinds of formation like imperatives and some questions. Get **it**?   75

Deep Structure, Surface Structure

John is eager to please and *John is easy to please*

Both sentences are "look-alike" – at the surface. We can even analyze them in an identical manner. In terms of underlying meaning – at a deeper level – we know they are different. The first implies that John pleases someone and the second that someone pleases John.

Similarly, a native speaker knows that *Sophie flew the kite* and *the kite was flown by Sophie* are different in syntactic form. According to traditional terminology, the first sentence is active and the second passive. However, at the underlying level, the two sentences share the same basic components. Sentences contain a manifest outer structure and a hidden, inner structure.

With this approach, to analyze a sentence grammatically means to show its **derivation**. There are two stages to this:

1. Apply the phrase structure rules. This opens up the **deep structure** of a sentence, an abstract level of organization where the basic syntactic relations are represented.

2. Apply transformation rules which change the deep structure of the sentence into the **surface structure**: that which is actually spoken.

The transformational subcomponent generates (assigns) a surface structure. Thus, det+N+V+det+N underlies a huge number of transitive sentences like *My brother chose the Burgundy*.

The subcomponent here can account for variants such as:
The Burgundy was chosen by my brother
The Burgundy was chosen
The choosing of the Burgundy (by my brother)
My brother's choosing of the Burgundy

Transformational Grammar (TG) is not an arrangement of examples or hints, but a *theory of language,* just as chemistry is a theory of other kinds of objects in the physical world. The far-reaching aim of TG is to point towards an understanding of the human mind. It constitutes an early attempt at the exploration of the properties common to all languages.

Note that the picture described here is about 30 years old, and would be accepted by few if any working linguists today.

Universal Grammar

In the theory known as **Universal Grammar** (UG), Chomsky explores the notion that there is in fact little variation among human languages. In doing so, he has tried to prepare the ground for a powerful theory of *first language acquisition.*

Universal grammar is not a grammar but a *state.*

One part of our biological make up is specifically dedicated to language. That is called our **language faculty**. UG is the **initial state** of that language faculty.

This initial language faculty is a device that yields a particular language when presented with the kind of evidence available to a child. The theory that deals with this system, the theory of the initial state (of the language acquisition device) is called universal grammar.

Universal grammar is that part of cognitive psychology (ultimately human biology) which seeks to determine the invariant principles of the language faculty and to determine as well the range of variation that those principles allow – that is, the *possible human languages.*

I HELD THAT ALL LANGUAGES SHARE IN COMMON THE SAME SUBSTANTIVE CATEGORIES (PARTS OF SPEECH) AND FORMAL CATEGORIES (SUBJECT AND PREDICATE).

ROGER BACON (C. 1214–94)

THE UNIVERSALIST VIEW FOUND ITS FULLEST EXPRESSION IN THE 17TH CENTURY WITH OUR **PORT-ROYAL GRAMMAR** OF 1660.

I DESCRIBED "INNER FORM", THAT IS, THE BASIC UNIVERSAL STRUCTURES UNDERLYING LANGUAGE. THIS FORESEES CHOMSKY'S "DEEP STRUCTURE".

HUMBOLDT

The human psyche is composed of innate forms always potentially present, giving direction and form to their actualization in images and action. The **collective unconscious** is universal; it is shared by everyone.

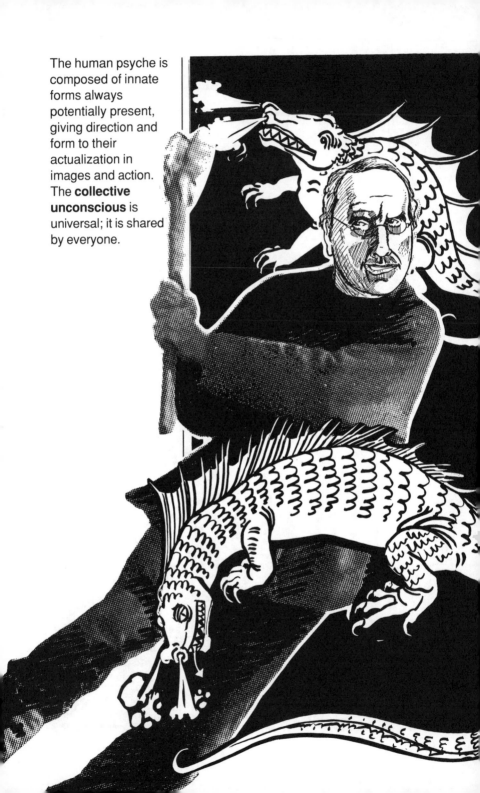

"THE AUTONOMIC CONTENTS OF THE UNCONSCIOUS OR 'DOMINANTS' . . . ARE NOT INHERITED IDEAS BUT INHERITED POSSIBILITIES, NECESSITIES EVEN, OF BRINGING TO BIRTH THE IDEAS BY WHICH THESE DOMINANTS HAVE BEEN EXPRESSED. EVERY REGION HAS ITS FORMS OF SPEECH, WHICH CAN VARY INFINITELY."

"But it matters little if the mythological hero overcomes now a dragon, now a fish or some other monster; the fundamental motive remains the same, and that is the common property of mankind, not the transitory formulations of different regions and periods. Thus, man is born with a complicated psychic precondition that is anything but a *tabula rasa* . . .
I have called the sphere of the general psychic inheritance the **collective unconscious**."
Carl Gustav Jung (1875-1961), lecture delivered in Karlsruhe, 1927.
In *Contributions to Analytical Psychology*, 1945.

81

Can We "Map" a Universal Grammar?

EVERY LINGUISTIC SYSTEM IS DISCRETE AND CONCRETE. DESCRIBE IT AS FULLY AS POSSIBLE, COMPREHENSIVELY, ELEGANTLY. MAP OUT ITS PHONOLOGY, MORPHOLOGY AND GRAMMATICAL STRUCTURE. TIE DOWN THE RELATION OF FORM TO FUNCTION. DO IT WITH GILYAK AND PESHTU, AS WELL AS FRENCH AND JAPANESE. THEN, AND ONLY THEN, IF THERE ARE LANGUAGE UNIVERSALS, YOU WILL SEE THEM EMERGE.

LANGUAGE UNIVERSALS

Not so. Comprehensiveness of coverage does not seem to me to be a serious or significant goal in the present stage of linguistic science. Rather, the central fact to which any significant linguistic theory must address itself is this: a mature speaker can produce . . .

Chomsky argued that we should find out what are the **borders** or **constraints** within which language operates. What is the **set of rules** underlying a language?

Universal grammar is not "a grammar". It is a theory which attempts to deal with questions about the general nature of language that were, in part, addressed in an earlier tradition but largely ignored (or sometimes dismissed as meaningless and absurd) in modern approaches.

Children's blueprint of language programmed into the mind-brain informs them how this internalized grammar works: **semantic rules** which help work out meaning, **phonological rules** which represent sound patterns, and then **syntactic rules** which are concerned with word arrangement.

How Does it Sound?

One of the main features of language is its so-called arbitrariness. The sounds which make up words are quite arbitrary choices. The English word *okay* can be *siguro* in Tagalog and *bien* in French. However, in UG it is the things that all languages have in common which reflect the human mind.

UG is a set of constraints on the construction of individual grammars. We construct a particular grammar as a result of the "triggering" experience in the environment. That is, our exposure to some natural language (French, Korean, etc.).

Empiricist Critics

Empiricists such as **John Locke** (1632–1704) and a philosopher of speech-act theory, **John Searle** (b. 1932), would say: "I'm not happy with this." Unconscious knowledge is conceptually absurd. Rules must be accessible to consciousness.

The Rule for Making Questions

To these empirical criticisms, Chomsky replies:

> There is no basis for an argument. I argue that the
> rules of grammar are mentally represented and employed
> in thought and behaviour. Let's take two examples. First,
> how do we form **questions**?

Take a *noun phrase* in any sentence. Replace it by the right *question-word*. Place the question-word at the *beginning* of the sentence. Do a few other mechanical things here and there, and abracadabra, you've got a question.

Suddenly, Patsy Rabbit saw Farmer Giles.

Oh no! Who did Patsy Rabbit suddenly see?

Now, let's make it a bit more complicated. Mother Rabbit doesn't deny that Farmer Giles' carrots taste good. But she warns all the little ones (especially Patsy), "No, no and no again!"

"Mr Sparrow thought that Mother Rabbit had warned all the little rabbits to keep away from Farmer Giles' garden."

Now question the little rabbits.

"Which rabbits did Mr Sparrow think that Mother Rabbit had told to keep away from the garden?"

"The carrots looked more delicious than Mother Rabbit had told the little rabbits they would be."

Here, if we question "the little rabbits" we get the sentence . . .

"Which rabbits were more delicious than Mother Rabbit had told that they would be?"

We know what we mean if we think hard enough. But as **a well-formed sentence** it won't do at all – except for Farmer Giles who likes rabbit pie.

Now working out such sentences involves a lot of complicated things – like blocking our perfectly normal inductive generalization to the ill-formed example (the last one). Surely, we have **not** had all the relevant training or experience to be able to do such things. Rather, a specific property of the human language faculty – something that derives from our modes of cognition – leads to this consequence.

The Rule for Reciprocal Expression

Now here's another example. How do we select **antecedents**?

Consider the phrase, "the men sit and hear each other."

Now a child knows that "each other" in English is a **reciprocal expression**. In other words, the expression "each other" must have something in front of it, connected to it, i.e. **an antecedent**.

You could place the antecedent in a different clause, as in: "the men want each other to hear the nightingale."

In the last sentence, "each other" is in a subordinate clause as the subject of "to hear", whereas its antecedent "the men" occurs in the main clause.

THE MEN WANT ME TO LISTEN TO EACH OTHER

However, sometimes the reciprocal loses its partner. It can't find its antecedent outside of its clause, as in: "the men want me to listen to each other."

This is not a well-formed sentence, but it has a sensible meaning: "each of the men wants me to listen to the other."

You might think that we can make a condition: the antecedent ought to be "the nearest Noun Phrase".

But not so. This condition is neither **sufficient**, as we see in the example, "the nightingales hoped that each other would sing" (if the condition were sufficient, then this would mean "each nightingale hoped that the other would sing", but it doesn't), nor **necessary**, as we see in the example, "the nightingales whistled songs at each other". Now, of course this could be interpreted as the nightingales whistled each song at the other song. But that is not the way we would normally interpret it.

89

A Theory of Scientific Theories?

Universal Grammar advances two radical proposals: that the complex structures of the mind-brain develop (1) from limited or **constrained evidence** and (2) in a **uniform way**. The theory locates itself in a truism about human nature: our capacities for organizing intelligible experiences of reality are **fixed**. What does this mean? It means that UG permits us to ask some important questions . . .

What is the science-forming capacity that enables us to recognize some theories as intelligible and natural, whilst rejecting others even if they are compatible with the evidence?

Is the human mind endowed with a set of principles which, when a certain plane of understanding particular questions is reached, then goes to work?

Do these principles – a general schematism which is an endowment of the mind – make possible the acquisition of rich systems of knowledge and belief?

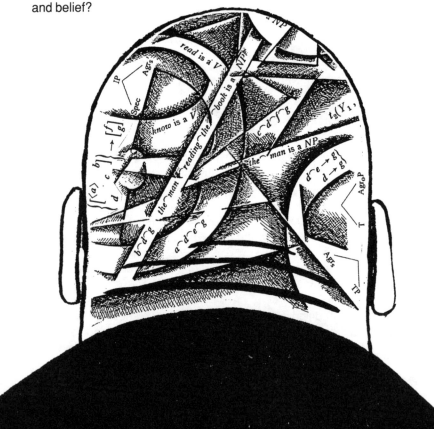

FREUD

By analyzing these principles, can we find out the **class of intelligible theories**? And this leads us to the crucial question. What is the relation between the class of humanly **accessible** theories and **true** theories?

This speculation on the laws of nature underpins the question of how and why we select some literary genres but not others, some ways of organizing sounds and not others. Not **every** organization of sound comprises a humanly accessible form of music. There seem to be constraints, conditions placed upon what is possible and what is not (i.e. what does not conform to normal human capacity).

Poetry, music, metaphor fall within and require a **general theory of symbolic function**. Freud attempted such a general theory. His formulation of psychoanalysis as a **theory of semiology** which could explain a joke, a painting, a myth, dreams, was an effort to uncover the abstract relation, in other words, various levels of representation between two systems: the surface or manifest organization of these phenomena and their latent deep-level structure.

Other Competing Models

From the 1960s, there was some shift of attention among developmental psychologists from Chomsky's generative model of Universal Grammar towards alternative explanations involving data-based investigation of children's spontaneous speech. Interest continued in the **developmental constructivism** of the Swiss psychologist **Jean Piaget** (1896–1980), whose theorizing about the capacities of pre-school children began in the 1920s. Piaget posited the existence of all-purpose cognitive skills switched on by regulatory and auto-regulatory mechanisms at each stage of the child's development. Piaget and his Geneva School argued that the child passes through a series of uniform stages, always following the same sequential order.

LANGUAGE ACQUISITION, IN OUR VIEW, OCCURS WITHIN THE CONTEXT OF INTELLECTUAL DEVELOPMENT AND EMERGES ONLY AFTER THE COGNITIVE FOUNDATIONS ARE ESTABLISHED.

THEREFORE, BEFORE CHILDREN CAN USE THE LINGUISTIC STRUCTURES OF COMPARISON, LIKE "MIFFY RABBIT IS BIGGER THAN MADELINE", THE CONCEPTUAL ABILITY TO MAKE *JUDGEMENTS OF SIZE* MUST HAVE BEEN DEVELOPED.

MOREOVER, LINGUISTIC DEVELOPMENT MIRRORS THE DEVELOPMENT OF SENSORI-MOTOR SKILLS.

Chomsky's Reply to Piaget

For Chomsky, the problem is that if one accepts the existence of
"cognitive stages", then how do such transitions take place?

Transition either results from
new information (which Piagetians deny)
or from some **intrinsic process of maturation**
(which they also deny).

Moreover, there is no known analogue to the principles of language
in other cognitive domains, so it is surely dogmatic to say simply that
linguistic development runs side by side with sensorimotor skills.

Other Linguistic Schools

WE'RE UNHAPPY WITH THE WAY GENERATIVE GRAMMAR "HIVES OFF" THE DAY-TO-DAY SOCIAL REALITY OF LANGUAGE.

FIRTH

HALLIDAY

In the 1960s, proponents of a new school of **Generative Semantics**, under **George Lakoff** (b. 1941), attempted to incorporate the notion that grammar also specified the social setting in which language is used. Generative Semanticists eventually dispersed into the various well-developed branches of sociolinguistics, e.g. semiotics, pragmatics, etc.

Robust alternatives to the generative model of language continued to flourish. An example was the **London School** founded by **John R. Firth** (1890–1960), reformulated in the neo-Firthian systemic-functional model of linguistics led by **M.A.K. Halliday** (b. 1925). Systemicists reject the notion of insulated, independent levels of analysis (morphology, phonology, syntax). Language, a social semiotic, consists of "polysystemic" language systems, comprising an infinite number of micro-systems of meaning-making which interact among the traditional levels of analysis.

1980s Minimalism

Looking for the smallest possible set of devices to account for language phenomena . . .

There are no superfluous elements in the phonology, semantics or syntax of human language. Everything serves a purpose and receives an appropriate interpretation. This is termed the **Full Interpretation** (FI) of language. It involves also a **Principle of Economy** (PE) whereby all representations of structures ought to be as **minimal** as possible, subject to something like a "least effort" condition.

MINIMALIST THEORY IS THE LATEST STAGE IN THE DEVELOPMENT OF PREVIOUS THEORIES. HOW WOULD YOU DESCRIBE IT?

It's not a theory. It's a programme.

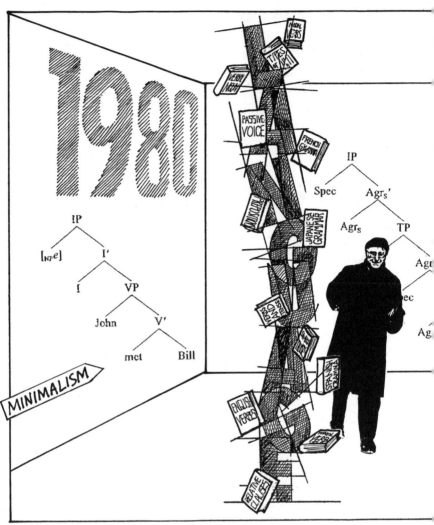

There was a big conceptual change in the field around 1980. A lot of things converged into something which really was a radical break with many centuries of traditional grammar – much more of a break than generative grammar. That's the "principles and parameters" approach. Traditional grammars are based on the idea that there are constructions like the "passive voice" or "relative clauses", and that each language has different rule systems for such constructions. This raised tremendous problems, and a good deal of research was designed to get round them.

Efforts finally converged around 1980 in a view which concluded that taxonomic categories like the "passive voice" were really **artefacts**, and what you really had were **fixed universal principles** which ran across all constructions in all languages. Points of variation had to do with very restricted parts of the lexicon – morphology, phonology. That approach was liberating. It led to a tremendous explosion in empirical research and to the radical exploration of things that we had not thought of. It was the first approach that made any **conceptual** sense.

How does the minimalist programme of "principles and parameters" work? Let's look at an example in practice.

Principles and Parameters

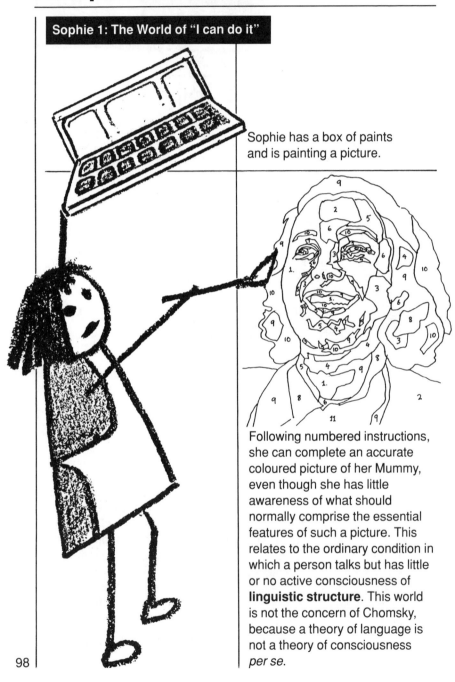

Sophie 1: The World of "I can do it"

Sophie has a box of paints and is painting a picture.

Following numbered instructions, she can complete an accurate coloured picture of her Mummy, even though she has little awareness of what should normally comprise the essential features of such a picture. This relates to the ordinary condition in which a person talks but has little or no active consciousness of **linguistic structure**. This world is not the concern of Chomsky, because a theory of language is not a theory of consciousness *per se*.

Now she has increased knowledge of what it is Mummy should look like and how such a picture ought to differ from Daddy, cats, rabbits and other things. This relates to the kind of knowing formulated in the theory of **transformational grammar**: knowledge of different types of sentences, how to disambiguate, how to distinguish between . . .

It is not difficult to find red peppers in Albuquerque
and
Red peppers are not difficult to find in Albuquerque

Sophie 3: The World of Basic Principles

This is the world of certain basic and highly general principles associated with the process of applying paints to a particular surface. The chemical reactions of this density of paint on that type of paper will have such and such a specific result. The molecular configuration of all blue colours combined with all kinds of green and H_2O will automatically result in this colour and viscosity.

SOPHIE, AND INDEED MOST PAINTERS, GET ALONG WELL ENOUGH WITHOUT THIS KNOWLEDGE. IT IS AN *UNDERLYING* KNOWLEDGE.

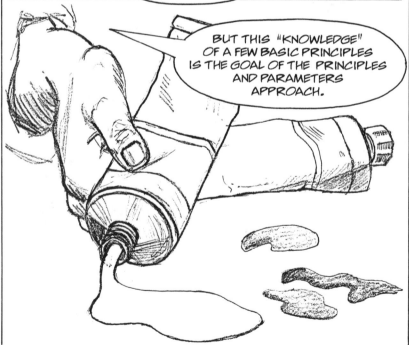

BUT THIS "KNOWLEDGE" OF A FEW BASIC PRINCIPLES IS THE GOAL OF THE PRINCIPLES AND PARAMETERS APPROACH.

The UG Principles and Parameters

Universal Grammar is a **computational system** that is rich and yet narrowly constrained in structure.

It contains **innate principles** determining what can and cannot happen.

It is rigid in its essential operations, with various transformations between the **surface structure** (S-structure) and the **deep structure** (D-structure).

It has a **modular structure**, i.e., it possesses separate components.

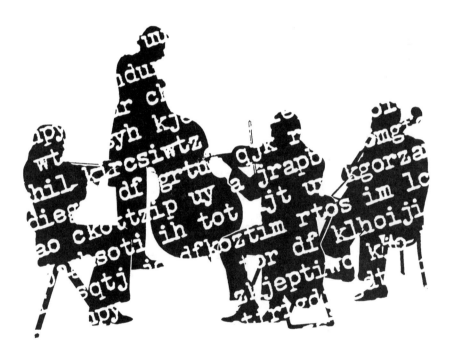

Like a string quartet comprising four instruments, each with its own separate constraints and functions, but whose output only "makes sense" when combined with the whole, the principles and parameters of this cognitive system are the main concern of this investigation.

Universal Grammar is not a grammar. Neither is it a theory of knowledge. It is a theory about the internal structure of the human mind.

Principles, therefore, are universal to all languages. The specific values for **parameters** are a fixed property of language which vary within very specific limits from one language to another.

For example, age, gender, and renal function are parameter values (*para* = in addition to) that determine blood pressure in the human body.

If renal function is damaged by an illness like diabetes, then the blood pressure goes up. Therefore the study of dietary salt intake by itself will not provide an accurate and complete picture of operating renal function.

In a tightly integrated theory with a fairly rich internal structure, change in a single parameter may have complex effects, with proliferating consequences in various parts of the grammar. *Chomsky*

Principles, Parameters and Language-Learning

Learning a language is fairly straightforward. It proceeds according to its own internal, predetermined course.

We view that problem of language acquisition as one of fixing parameters in a largely determined system. *Chomsky*

To learn a language means to learn how the Principles apply to a particular language, like the value attached to each Parameter.

Take for instance the notion of **Head Parameter**. This means that the essential part of a phrase is its **Head**.

Thus the noun phrase (NP)
pictures of Alice
has a head noun *pictures*.

The prepositional phrase
on my blue guitar
has a head preposition *on*.

The verb phrase (VP)
ride a bicycle
has a head verb *ride*.

Limited Variation

If we look at how head words function in relation to other workings of the phrase (complements), not all languages appear to be the same. In Japanese, unlike English, the preposition *de* appears on the right of the complement *blue guitar*.

It is likely that we can generalize across all human languages regarding the position of heads in phrases. Languages are either **head-first** (like English with its verbs on the left) or **head-last** (like Japanese with its verbs on the right).

In this way, **variation** across language can be explained by examining the limited choice (in fact only one) in **head parameters** that children have.

Ideally, we hope to find that complexes of properties differentiating otherwise similar languages are reducible to a single parameter, fixed in one way or another. *Chomsky*

Objection

WHY THEN DO WE ALL SPEAK **DIFFERENT** LANGUAGES? WHY IS THERE NOT ONE HUMAN LANGUAGE ONLY?

The reason is that Universal Grammar is only **partially** wired up.

We may think of UG as an intricately structured system, but one that is only partially "wired up". The system is associated with a finite set of switches, each of which has a finite number of positions (perhaps two). Experience is required to set the switches. When they are set, the system functions. *Chomsky*

Within the various modules, there are option points. You can go this way or that way. Based on evidence in the environment, a switch is set in a particular direction.

Accounting for Language

CHOMSKY:

There are two big problems that you have to meet to account for the properties of language, and these seem to go in opposite directions.

One is to get the facts straight – what's called **descriptive adequacy**: if the language does X, you need to account for it. The pursuit of getting the facts straight seems to lead to exceedingly complex and varied rule systems. From the other point of view, there is the opposite problem. You have to show that all languages are basically **identical**. That has got to be the case, because although children don't have much evidence, they learn it all the same. Languages have to be identical for the same reason that the human form or the circulatory system is identical. Each differs a little from person to person, but the uniformity is overwhelming.

Every biologist just assumes that the basic character of the circulatory system is an expression of the genes. For the same reason, we have to assume that all language is a basic expression of the genes. And so, on the one hand, all languages are pretty similar, although some parts are better understood than others. On the other hand, they all look terribly varied, complex, with rule systems different from one another.

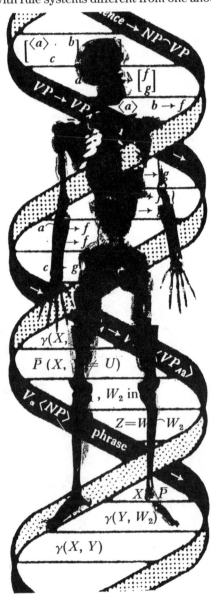

The conflict between these two opposite conclusions became very evident as soon as the first attempts were made to take traditional grammars and dictionaries and overcome the hand-waving (it's mostly hand-waving – a few hints here and there in what are called "primers" or "dictionaries"). If you try to fill in the gaps, they turn out to cause more problems. Well, the principles and parameters gave a possible answer to that – a way of thinking about language.

You can start by asking the kinds of questions that are often not asked in the sciences. You can ask whether specific descriptive devices that are used are really justified empirically, or are just engineering tricks to paper over a lack of understanding. Do you really have an independent justification for those devices, or are you using them because you don't know what's really going on and you have to describe it somehow? The way you might build a bridge without understanding fundamental physics. You can use tricks. And in fact most of the sciences, even the hard sciences, use plenty of tricks, because it's too difficult to show how every conceptual step can be justified.

The minimalist programme begins with such questions. It takes off from the **principles-parameters** approach.

Dispensable Technology

One pillar of the minimalist programme is the speculation that these are quite reasonable questions to ask, and the pursuit of them has been fairly fruitful. A lot of the things that were assumed to be necessary – to be parts of language – if you analyze them closely, turn out to be dispensable technology. You've often got better empirical results with conceptually more minimal assumptions.

The other part of the minimalist programme is much more controversial. Maybe it's premature, but there's some answer to the question of what's **real** and what's being used to paper over a **lack of understanding**. Maybe it's way in the future, but there's some answer to that.

A Fairy Tale

There's another question which may not have an answer. It would be kind of surprising if it did. I can explain it most easily by telling a sort of fairy tale about evolution.

There's a primate around with the same sensorimotor apparatus that we have, and the same conceptual apparatus. It thinks our thoughts but doesn't have language ability. So it thinks our thoughts as much as it can without language. It has our intentions and goals. It has our articulatory tools and our perceptual apparatus. It's just missing our **language faculty**.

Then some event takes place. It could be cosmic rays. Some mutation takes place and it reorganizes the brain in such a fashion as essentially to leave the sensorimotor apparatus, the conceptual apparatus, the intentional apparatus (how to refer to, to talk about, expect to do) unchanged, but it inserts a **language faculty**. Well, what might that language faculty look like? Suppose that it was optimally designed. Suppose a divine designer invented it. Call it a perfect language faculty. What would it be like?

There is one property that it has to have. The language faculty provides linguistic expressions, like the ones I'm using. Those linguistic expressions have to be "legible" to the other systems of the brain. For example, the sensorimotor apparatus has to make some sense out of it, otherwise I can't make noises. I can't externalize what I'm doing. It doesn't interface with the sensorimotor system. Whatever parts of the brain are there, this system has to provide instructions to them. Well, here is a perfect language faculty whose design is the best possible solution to the interface requirement.

The Simplest Possible System?

Instructions about **sound** or instructions about **meaning**: that's a minimal aspect of language. You assume our primate has it. Okay, now we ask: let's suppose that you wanted the least possible apparatus to provide expressions that on the one hand would yield instructions for the sensorimotor system, and on the other yield expressions for the conceptual-intentional system. Here we move into a delicate area of "What's the simplest possible system?" We have some ideas about that.

In fact, these ideas are used constantly in rational inquiry. Certainly in the natural sciences. It is ideas of that kind that make physicists unhappy if they discover seven elementary particles. Seven is not a nice enough number. They want it to be two or three. What drives human rational inquiry has been astonishingly successful in some parts of the sciences. So let's assume that it continues to work, for whatever mysterious reason.

The Perfect Design

Well, the other part of the minimalist programme is the expectation, the suspicion if you like, that language is **perfectly designed**. The imperfections and departures from optimally satisfying these two conditions are extremely limited. They are probably there for some good reason. Something to do with interpretation and so on. Now that need not be true. The language faculty might be very **badly** designed. In fact, everything in an organism is badly designed from some point of view. There is no such thing as "perfect design".

That's just normal. It's the way evolution works. It does the best it can with a bad set of tools. It would be pretty surprising if you found an organ which was perfectly designed for a very limited requirement. In fact, that's much less than is traditionally assumed in the study of language. If you study language, you try to look at sound-meaning correlations. But if you follow this approach, even sound-meaning correlations are too much data. It should be enough just to look at sound and meaning independently, with the sound-meaning correlations falling out from the basic design properties – quite an awesome project, and far from achievement.

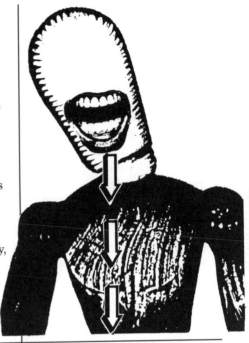

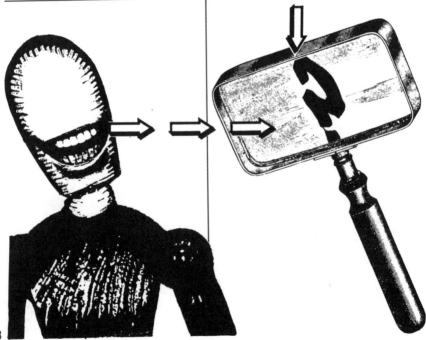

It's an awful lot to ask. The idea that "perfect design" might hold of language is very far-reaching. It would be a very surprising discovery about a biological system, which would mean one of two things: either this is a very unusual system or else we misunderstand biological systems generally. Either way, it would be quite interesting if it were true.

Insofar as the notion "simple" is clear for any science, there's no reason to doubt that the question of what's the simplest system will have an answer (whether we can find it or not). The minimalist programme is about a completely different matter: (1) whether it is appropriate now to ask far-reaching questions about "dispensable technology"; and (2) whether it is at all reasonable to suppose that language might have something approaching "perfect design". The first question might well be premature; it commonly is, in empirical inquiry. The second might be completely off the wall.

Incidentally, how crazy is this fairy tale about evolution? Pretty crazy. But it might be less crazy than most of the speculations about evolution of higher mental processes. Something roughly like it might turn out to be correct.

The Origins of a Social Conscience

Avram Noam Chomsky was born on 7 December 1928 in Philadelphia, Pennsylvania, USA. His father William Chomsky (1897–1976), a noted Hebrew scholar, emigrated from Russia in 1913 to avoid being drafted into the Tsarist army. Chomsky attended a Deweyite progressive school. As a boy during the Great Depression (1929–39), Chomsky was much affected by the violent strike-breaking, the desperation and humiliation of working people.

Just after my 10th birthday,
I wrote an editorial for my school newspaper
on the Fall of Barcelona at the close of
the Spanish Civil War (1936–39).

Chomsky was influenced by the richness and intensity of Jewish intellectual life in New York, which he visited by train. He haunted the Fourth Avenue second-hand bookshops, the office of the anarchist press *Freie Arbeiter Stimme,* and became intrigued by libertarian ideas.

At the corner of 72nd Street and Broadway was a kiosk run by Chomsky's uncle. It didn't sell many newspapers but it served as a rendezvous for European émigrés and Jewish working class intellectuals, poor, slum-dwellers, but rich in culture.

We'd hang out all night and have discussions and arguments, there or in his small apartment nearby. The great moments of my life in those years were when I could work at the news-stand at night and listen to all this.

Chomsky viewed the emergence of Fascism in Europe, and the anti-Semitic support for it in the streets at home. He was sceptical of the patriotic interpretation of the Second World War. Although rigorously anti-Nazi, he was appalled by the treatment of German POWs in the camp next to his High School.

It was generally considered the red-blooded thing to abuse them across the barbed-wire.

I remember on the day of the Hiroshima bombing I literally couldn't talk to anybody. I walked off into the woods and stayed alone for a couple of hours . . . I could never talk to anyone about it and never understood anyone's reaction. I felt completely isolated.

At the University of Pennsylvania, Chomsky studied with **Zellig S. Harris**, teacher of linguistics, with whose libertarian views (a "semi-anarchist strain") he had political affinity. Chomsky's early work grows directly out of Harris' work.

123

A Chomsky File

1949. Marries the linguist Carol Schatz. They have one son and two daughters. His undergraduate thesis, *Morphophonemics of Modern Hebrew*, was a first attempt to construct a generative grammar.

1951–55. Junior Fellow of the Harvard University Society of Fellows.

1955. Completes doctoral dissertation entitled *Transformational Analysis* and receives his Ph.D. in linguistics. Mimeograph of *The Logical Structure of Linguistic Theory* in circulation. Joins the staff of the Massachusetts Institute of Technology (MIT) in Cambridge, Boston.

1957. The major theoretical viewpoints of the dissertation appear in the monograph *Syntactic Structure*.

1961. Appointed full professor in the MIT Department of Modern Languages and Linguistics (now the Department of Linguistics and Philosophy).

1965. Organizes citizens' committee to publicize tax refusal as a protest against the war in Vietnam.

1966. Becomes Ferrari Ward Professor of Linguistics at MIT.

1969. Delivers the John Locke Lectures at Oxford University. Publishes his first book on political issues, *American Power and the New Mandarins*.

1970. Delivers the Bertrand Russell Memorial Lecture at Cambridge University.

1972. Nehru Memorial Lecture in New Delhi.

1976. Appointed Institute Professor.

1977. Huizinga Lecture in Leiden.

1986. The Managua Lectures, Universidad Centroamericana, Nicaragua. Fellow of the American Academy of Arts and Sciences and the National Academy of Science. Honorary degrees from the University of London, Loyola University of Chicago, Georgetown University, Swarthmore College, Delhi University, Cambridge University and others.

Chomsky the Social Critic

Chomsky is internationally renowned as a consistent critic of social injustices. In brief, his social philosophy makes clear

– how the institutions of authority and power enforce control over
  populations
– how intellectuals have betrayed their conscience and community and
  have been co-opted to serve state power

Chomsky's criticism of US foreign policy in particular has unmasked

– the pervasive violence of US imperial policy around the world
– the omnipresent and manufactured self-image of the US as
  well-intentioned and "essentially benign"
– the manipulation of reality that flows from self-righteousness
– the poverty and disrepair of American democracy

"Is What You Say True?"

Chomsky rejects any personalization of social issues. For this reason, he denies a necessary link between his linguistic and social views, because one thing does not depend on the other, and to argue that they do is dangerous.

You don't need specialist training in linguistics to be capable of condemning US support for atrocities in East Timor. It shouldn't matter who's speaking, their background or "qualifications" for saying it. What matters is the question: "Is what you say **true**?"

I CAN THINK FOR MYSELF.

Nevertheless, one can see an important relation between language (*what* it is) and human freedom (*how* language is used).

The Tower of Babel

The Tower of Babel is a Biblical symbol of humans divided by language, but language differences are a source of richness and need not be the cause of pain or confusion. Conflict is caused instead by other factors, such as group identification and chauvinism.

Universal grammar, properly understood, contributes to the understanding that the human race is united as a species by overwhelming similarities.

We can help eliminate divisions, not by imposing linguistic and cultural uniformity, but rather by addressing the reasons why people live unequal and painful lives.

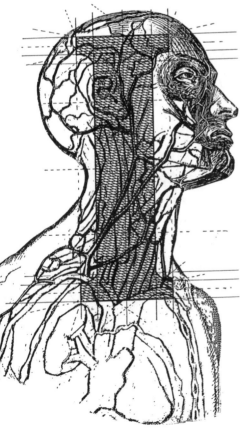

It is reasonable to suppose that just as intrinsic structures of mind underlie the development of cognitive structures, so a "species character" provides the framework for the growth of moral consciousness, cultural achievement and even participation in a free and just community. It is, to be sure, a great intellectual leap from observation on the basis for cognitive development to particular conclusions on the laws of our nature and the conditions for their fulfilment; say, to the conclusion that human needs and capacities will find their fullest expression in a society of free and creative producers, working in a system of free association in which "social bonds" will replace "all fetters in human society".
Chomsky

Chomsky is making two interrelated points. The uniformity of languages is a human genetic inheritance based on immutable biological principles. Language is nevertheless free-standing and able to withstand the powerful pressures of the environment. So also, human nature at its deepest level is resistant to the winds of social forces.

> Oppressive political systems
> can never ultimately control our minds.
> We are free men and women.

Here a link between a philosophy of language and a philosophy of anarchism begins to emerge.

Chomsky's Libertarian Inheritance

Chomsky's social philosophy inherits a long tradition of libertarian thinking. One of his inspirational figures is the educationalist **Wilhelm von Humboldt** (1767–1835), a founder of the University of Berlin, chief architect of the Prussian educational system and a critic of the authoritarian state.

> Humboldt was one of the most profound theorists of general linguistics and also an early advocate of libertarian values.

Humboldt's educational philosophy is based on the idea of *Bildung* (formation), a faculty which progressively develops the person and is present as much in the species as in the individual.

ALL MORAL CULTURE SPRINGS SOLELY AND IMMEDIATELY FROM THE INNER LIFE OF THE SOUL, AND CAN ONLY BE STIMULATED IN HUMAN NATURE, AND NEVER PRODUCED BY EXTERNAL AND ARTIFICIAL CONTRIVANCES.

Another of Chomsky's heroes is **John Dewey** (1859–1952), American philosopher, psychologist, educator and social critic. Dewey was a pioneer of the progressive school movement. His essay *The Reflex Arc Concept in Psychology*, on the adjustment of the total organism to the environment, heralded the beginning of functional psychology.

I think Humboldt would have found congenial much of Dewey's thinking about education.

A vigorous social critic of US domestic and foreign policy, Dewey became active, whilst Professor of Philosophy at Chicago University, in fighting the exploitation of immigrant and minority groups in the Chicago slums, supporting legislation to legalize unions and attacking the role of corporate power.

I ACCUSE CONGRESS AND THE POLITICAL ESTABLISHMENT OF BEING THE ERRAND BOYS OF BIG BUSINESS!

Adam Smith's "Vile Maxim"

Chomsky also refers to **Adam Smith** (1723–90), a Scottish philosopher and economist of the Enlightenment period. Smith's criticism of early capitalism has been shamelessly distorted by British Thatcherite conservatives into a defence of the "free market".

Smith condemned mercantilism and colonialism as harmful to the people generally but of great benefit to the merchants and manufacturers who were the "principal architects" of state policy, and whose interests were "most peculiarly attended to" . . .

Adam Smith's lesson holds true as we move on to the modern era, often applying, in an internationalized economy, even after military defeat. Consider, for example, how the interests of the Nazi collaborators in the corporate and financial worlds were "most peculiarly attended to" as the US occupation restored them to their proper place.

Enlightenment Values

20th century libertarian values can be traced back to the 18th century Enlightenment, a radical philosophical movement which championed rationalism, individual liberty and progress. Chomsky is heir to the Enlightenment spirit of liberal thinking. Just as the libertarian **Jean-Jacques Rousseau** (1712–78) reformulated the ideas of Descartes into a philosophy of social justice (***Discourse on Inequality***, 1754), so also Chomsky follows on from this Cartesian tradition.

The essentials of human freedom are set out in the Cartesian theses . . .

1. Introspection discloses to you that you indeed have a mind.
2. The essence of this mind is thought itself.
3. Language is a creative substance.
4. Freedom of thought can only be grounded in the creative use of language.
5. This creativity must be able to think new thoughts, prove to be free of stimuli and therefore utterly innovative, coherent and appropriate to situations.
6. Since we know that other organisms use language in a creative manner, we must attribute them with a mind like ours.

A modern version of Enlightenment thinking can be found in **libertarian socialism** or **anarchism** (the terms are interchangeable).

DESCARTES

ROUSSEAU

Anarchism

Anarchism or libertarian socialism is not a doctrine. It is a fundamentally non-hierarchical way of thinking, acting and relating to other people. Anarchist theory comprehends various strands: libertarian socialism, anarcho-syndicalism and communist anarchism.

The shape of society envisaged by anarchism is of one organically composed of small communities centring on two units: the neighbourhood and the workplace.

THE LIBERTARIAN SOCIALIST WISHES TO SEE CENTRALIZED STATE OR ECONOMIC POWER DIFFUSED AND UNDER THE CONTROL OF COOPERATIVE PARTICIPANTS.

SUCH EVIDENCE AS THERE IS SHOWS THAT WORKERS' CONTROL INCREASES EFFICIENCY.

BUT CAPITALISTS DON'T WANT IT. WE'RE WORRIED ABOUT *CONTROL* - NOT PRODUCTIVITY OR EFFICIENCY.

And Liberalism?

What about "liberalism"? Does it not have a part to play in the reform of society?

THERE IS MUCH REFERENCE IN POLITICAL TALK IN AMERICA TO "OUR LIBERAL TRADITION". WHAT'S GOING ON WITH THIS TERM "LIBERAL"?

Meanings have become so destroyed you can barely talk. "Liberal" here means the opposite of what it used to mean. "Conservative"? There is no conservative tradition in the United States in the sense of British Toryism. There is a tradition of reactionary statism. Liberal means New Deal-ish, very mildly social democratic. Now we see an effort to roll back the social contract and return to the good ol' roaring 1920s before we had to worry about workers' rights. There has been an unravelling of the social contract both in the United States and Britain. Even this kind of liberalism is passé. We now have a perfection of the principle of dog-eat-dog, devil take the hindmost.

Action Intellectuals

THERE'S A PARTICULAR STRAIN OF DESIGNER-BUILT POLITICIAN, AVOWEDLY "LIBERAL", WHICH HAS A PECULIAR FASCINATION FOR SOME. I THINK THIS IS WHAT YOU TERM "ACTION INTELLECTUAL"? WHAT OR WHO IS AN "ACTION INTELLECTUAL"?

ROBERT McNAMARA

It's not my term. The group around Kennedy described themselves as "action intelluals", the people who went down to Washington to found Camelot. Not the kind of reflective type who sits around the Faculty Club but "real intellectuals". They are the smart guys who are going to take charge and run the world – nicely. They are very similar to the Leninist commissars. In fact, I've done some comparisons of things written by, say, MacNamara and Lenin. They are remarkably similar. In fact, the ideology is similar.

The American Paradox

The United States proudly styles itself "the leader of the Free World". We know the US as a free and open society, more so in many ways than societies in Western Europe. And yet, Chomsky has criticized the US as blind to what it really is . . .

1. One of the most depoliticized nations in the industrial world
2. One of the most deeply indoctrinated societies in the industrial world
3. One of the most conformist intelligentsias in the industrial world

The freer the society the more well-honed
and sophisticated its system of thought control
and indoctrination. The ruling élite, clever, class-conscious,
ever sure of domination, make sure of that.

Remedy? Cartesian common-sense. To see through the forest of endless
deceit in which people have become entangled. And people can do it.
They have first to make the effort.

Let's see how it has been possible to achieve depoliticization,
indoctrination and intellectual conformism in the self-crowned "leader of
the Free World".

The Manufacture of Consent

One way of achieving control is by apparently gaining the agreement of the people.

I COINED THE PHRASE "THE MANUFACTURE OF CONSENT" TO DESCRIBE THIS ESSENTIAL COERCIVE FEATURE OF AMERICAN-STYLE DEMOCRACY.

You cannot force people to obey by violence, as the Soviet system tried to do. So you need systems of indoctrination to ensure that they agree to what the ruling groups want to do.

Walter Lippman (1889–1974) editor, writer and formidable columnist of the *New York Herald-Tribune*, in **Public Opinion**, 1922.

Some changes did take place at the end of the 60s in the universities, largely due to the student movement, which demanded and achieved some broadening of the tolerated range of thinking. The reactions have been interesting. Now that the pressure of the student movement has been reduced, there is substantial effort to reconstruct the orthodoxy that had been slightly disturbed. And constantly, in the discussions and literature dealing with that period – often called "the time of troubles" or something of that sort – the student left is depicted as a menace threatening freedom of research and teaching; the student movement is said to have placed the freedom of the universities in jeopardy by seeking to impose totalitarian ideological controls. That is how the state capitalist intellectuals describe the fact that their near-total control of ideology was very briefly brought into question. *Chomsky*

Smash the Unions!

The central institutions of capitalist society are under the autocratic control of corporations and industries. A corporation or industry, considered in political terms, is hierarchically fascist: tight control at the top and strict obedience at every level. There is some bargaining, a little give and take, but the line of authority is straightforward.

GOVERNMENT IS THE SHADOW CAST BY BUSINESS OVER SOCIETY.
JOHN DEWEY

The most effective democratizing force in such a society is the labour movement. You can measure the strength of this democratic force by the sustained, sophisticated and often violent efforts to control or destroy it altogether.

We now see, at the millennium, a globalizing free market which is intent on undermining the self-help societies of working people, i.e., the unions. Unions are portrayed as something that workers have to fight against. The message is explicit: "Free yourselves from the oppression of the unions!" How can this be done?

1. Promote social science frauds like the importance of "harmony" in the workplace.
2. Disseminate the view that unionism is anti-American.
3. Enter the school system and educate the nation's future workforce towards right-mindedness. (By the 1950s, one-third of all school textbooks were being provided by corporations.)
4. Circulate glossy magazines for students to learn the right way to money and power and the management of the lesser-educated working people.
5. Flood the media, schools, churches, entertainment industry with propaganda about the right American values.

Class and Poverty

In 1994, the Census Bureau reported that the number of Americans earning less than poverty-level incomes rose by 50% over the last decade. Income inequality in the US is worse than in any other industrialized country in the world – surpassing even Britain.

American blacks, we know, have shorter life expectancy, higher infant mortality rates and poorer quality of life – Third World statistics. But what happens if you employ the factors of **class** and race and re-analyze these statistics?

Every major medical journal in the US refused to publish Navarro's findings. They were finally accepted by the world's leading medical journal, *The Lancet*, in Britain.

Who Do You Blame?

Things are wrong. There is anger. But blaming the government can be a form of depoliticization.

GOVERNMENT IS THE ONE INSTITUTION YOU *CAN* CHANGE. IT HAS A DEFECT – IT'S POTENTIALLY DEMOCRATIC.

AH, BUT CORPORATIONS HAVE NO SUCH DEFECT. THEY ARE TYRANNIES. SO KEEP CORPORATIONS INVISIBLE AND FOCUS YOUR ANGER ON THE GOVERNMENT.

If you don't like something or your wages are going down – blame the government. You don't blame the guys in the *Fortune 500* because you don't read the *Fortune 500*.

For some, Marxism provided a theoretical model for what's really going on. But what's happened to Marxism?

HAS MARX INFLUENCED YOUR CONCEPTION OF CAPITALIST SOCIETY AND SOCIAL THEORY? I THINK THIS IS RELEVANT ON ACCOUNT OF THE SO-CALLED "DEMISE OF MARXISM" THESE DAYS.

WAGE-LABOUR AND CAPITAL.

By KARL MARX.

WITH INTRODUCTION BY FREDERICK ENGELS

I'm not a big Marxologist. Marx had a theory of capitalism. You can read it for whatever interest it has. A lot. He had nothing to say about a post-capitalist society. Only about five sentences.

Marx had no conception of socialism. He simply argued that capitalism was going to change in certain directions. Having said that, there is no way you can say that Marxism has had its "demise". It's conceptually impossible. It has had its "demise" if you don't like his theory of capitalism. Certainly an intelligent person should read it and learn from it. It has its flaws. It was temporally bounded. It didn't come from God.

The Fall of the Soviet Empire

WITH THE COLLAPSE OF THE SOVIET EMPIRE AND THE NEAR ECSTASY WITH WHICH THE WEST HAS GREETED THE HEGEMONY OF THE UNITED STATES, IT IS FASHIONABLE NOW TO SPEAK OF THE "DEMISE OF SOCIALISM".

The demise of socialism? That's very interesting. It shows how propaganda systems work. In 1917, at the time of the Bolshevik take-over, every socialist institution of the pre-coup period was instantly destroyed. The factory councils and the soviets that had formed effectively disappeared. Lenin and Trotsky were orthodox Marxists of a certain kind. They probably didn't think a socialist revolution was possible in this backward peasant society. They would wait for the iron laws of history to grind out a revolution in Germany, the capitalist country next door. It didn't work that way. There was an uprising, supported with great misgivings by honest revolutionaries like Rosa Luxemburg. But it was crushed. And so there they were, Lenin and Trotsky, in this deeply impoverished peasant society. The original poor Third World society from the 15th century.

The first thing they did was to move to state capitalism. From that point on, the Russian system, particularly as it developed under Stalin, described itself with two words: "democratic" and "socialist". Western propaganda of course ridiculed the claim that Eastern bloc countries were democratic, but it loved the claim that they were socialist. It was very useful to say, "Yes, that's socialism." You could associate socialism with this very backward Third World society which was being driven towards industrialization by violence and in many ugly ways. Identify that with socialism and you obtain a very powerful weapon to defeat attempts to extend freedom and justice in your own society. There certainly was a destruction of socialism, but that took place in 1917–18. A totalitarian state-society has now dissolved. It is an opportunity to extend freedom.

149

WHERE IS FREEDOM NOW?

Russia is being driven right back to the Third World where it came from. The universal conclusion in the West, left or right, is that Russia was an economic failure. What is this based on? Well, the usual argument is: "Just look at Western and Eastern Europe. One is a success and the other a failure!" That makes about as much sense as looking at the kindergartens in Boston and saying: "They're a total failure! Compare the amount of quantum physics that those kids know with the students at MIT graduate school." If you want to find out how good kindergartens are, you compare them with other kindergartens, not with MIT graduate school.

To make a serious comparison, try Russia and Brazil. They're reasonably close: two big countries rich in resources, one of them subjected to the Leninist-Stalinist system and the other to our system, a Western colony. The US took it over in 1945, has been running it ever since and is very proud of it. Actually, it's not a completely fair comparison. Brazil has had many advantages that Russia hasn't had. Brazil was never subjected to destructive world wars. It had the supposed advantage of Western tutelage. Let's make the comparison anyway. How does it come out? 10% of Brazil's population is better off than Russia's. But for 80–90% of the people of Brazil, it's a total disaster. They would regard the conditions of Eastern Europe as an attainable dream. Compare Guatemala and Bulgaria. Any reasonable comparison is bound to yield similar conclusions. The Leninist-Stalinist system is catastrophic enough, but the Western system is even more catastrophic. Now, that is not a popular conclusion. The "rational" explanation is totally absurd. People would laugh at it, if they weren't so brainwashed.

Who Should Apologize?

JAPAN HAS COME IN FOR INTERNATIONAL CRITICISM OVER ITS "FAILURE TO APOLOGIZE PROPERLY" FOR THE INVASION AND OCCUPATION OF ASIA AND SUBSEQUENT BRUTALITIES DURING THE COLONIAL PERIOD. WHAT IS YOUR VIEW ON THIS?

This is curious, because the Japanese have gone way beyond what we have. When they do apologize, that's always a front-page story – "the Japanese didn't quite do it right". These same critics in the US would never dream of apologizing for US atrocities. The United States doesn't recognize the concept of war guilt. It's as if the French, the Dutch, the English and the Americans never carried out any crime. And of course we didn't. We don't admit that we carried out crimes, so we didn't.

American history begins with the slaughter of defenceless people – the Pequot native Americans in the 1600s, right here in Massachusetts. Massacre is bad for the character. And it's been going on: the terrorist wars of Central America, the wars in Indochina. *It wouldn't occur to anyone to apologize.*

Robert MacNamara wrote a book which was supposed to have been an apology for the US war in Indochina. He apologized to the American people because a lot of Americans got killed, it had disrupted American society. But that doesn't constitute a word of apology.

Robert MacNamara,
US Secretary of Defence under
President Lyndon B. Johnson

Remembering Vietnam

There was US support for the French attempt to reconquer their colony of Vietnam after the Japanese occupation of Indochina in World War II. In 1954, the Geneva Conference ended French control of territories in Indochina, but the US disrupted this peace process by establishing a terrorist régime in South Vietnam. When it began to look shaky, President Kennedy in 1962 dispatched the US Air Force to attack rural South Vietnam where over 80% of the population lived. Civilian targets were bombed and defoliation began.

President Kennedy also instigated a campaign to place several million people into concentration camps – known as "strategic hamlets" – surrounded by barbed-wire and guards.

This was in order to protect them from the Viet Cong guerrillas whom the population *supported*, as the US itself conceded.

The US resisted attempts at a peace settlement and in 1964 planned the ground invasion of South Vietnam, which took place early in 1965. Intensified bombing of the South rose to triple the level of the more publicized attack on the North. This gruesome and pointless war went on until 1975.

Overcoming the "Vietnam Syndrome"

WE HAVE NO NEED TO APOLOGIZE OR CASTIGATE OURSELVES OR ASSUME THE STATUS OF CULPABILITY. WE DO NOT OWE A DEBT. OUR INTENTIONS WERE TO DEFEND THE FREEDOMS OF THE SOUTH VIETNAMESE, AND THE DESTRUCTION WAS MUTUAL.
PRESIDENT JIMMY CARTER, NEWS CONFERENCE, 1977

If the Nuremberg laws were applied, then every post-war American president would have been hanged.

The point has been to get over the "Vietnam Syndrome". This can be defined as a form of PTSD (post-traumatic stress disorder), experienced on a mass scale in the US, resulting from revulsion over the Indochina experience of the 1960s. What are its psychological symptoms?

SICKLY INHIBITIONS AGAINST THE USE OF MILITARY FORCE . . .

NORMAN PODHORETZ, NEO-CONSERVATIVE EDITOR OF **COMMENTARY**

Its physical effects impede the ability to exercise proper US control of its dependencies.

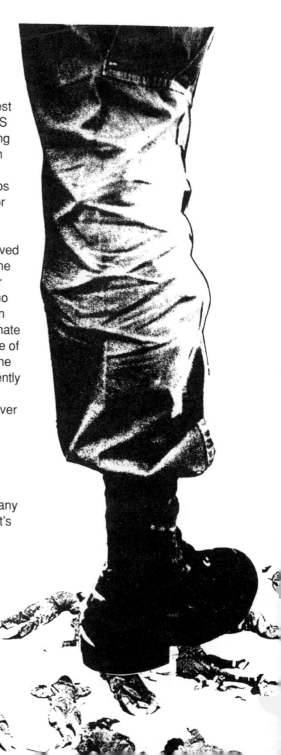

Treatment

1. The flooding technique, i.e. more of the same ("military aggression") but in a safe environment.

Example. The glorious conquest of Grenada when 6,000 élite US troops succeeded in overcoming the resistance of several dozen Cubans and some Grenadan militiamen. The American troops won 8,000 medals of honour for their prowess.

2. Present the US as the aggrieved party and the Vietnamese as the aggressors. Focus on the bitter memories of the Americans who suffered from the war. Focus on the lack of good will of the obstinate Vietnamese concerning the fate of the "boat people". Stress that the Vietnamese have been insufficiently forthcoming on the remains of American soldiers shot down over Vietnam.

3. NEVER apologize. NEVER admit culpability.

But Vietnam was just one of many victims of US foreign policy. Let's examine two more cases: **Indonesia** and **Nicaragua**.

The Indonesia-East Timor File

After Japanese occupation in World War II, Indonesia became a republic in 1945 under the nationalist leadership of **Dr Sukarno** (1901–70), and gained independence from the Netherlands in 1949–50. Sukarno was viewed with suspicion by US experts on South East Asia.

A US-sponsored armed insurrection against Sukarno in 1957–58 failed, but was followed by a classic destabilization policy of supporting and training the Indonesian military. This finally bore fruit in the military coup of 1965–66 which deposed Sukarno. Pro-US **General Suharto** (b. 1921) came to power after a bloodbath.

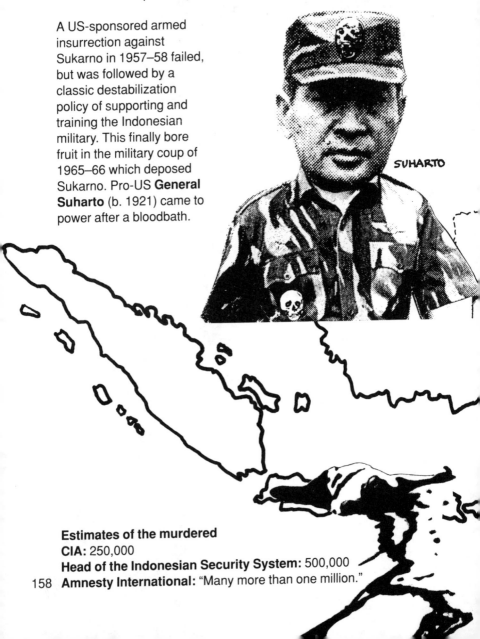

SUHARTO

Estimates of the murdered
CIA: 250,000
Head of the Indonesian Security System: 500,000
158 **Amnesty International:** "Many more than one million."

East Timor

The Indonesian military régime's occupation of the former Portuguese colony of East Timor in 1975 is a near-genocidal event.

Daniel Patrick Moynihan, the US ambassador to the UN, takes pride in blocking any international reaction to the mass slaughter. He explains helpfully that only within a few weeks, 60,000 people were killed: "10% of the population, almost the proportion of the casualties experienced by the Soviet Union during the Second World War."

THE UNITED STATES WISHED THINGS TO TURN OUT AS THEY DID AND WORKED TO BRING THIS ABOUT. THE DEPARTMENT OF STATE DESIRED THAT THE UNITED NATIONS PROVE UTTERLY INEFFECTIVE IN WHATEVER MEASURES IT UNDERTOOK. THIS TASK WAS GIVEN TO ME, AND I CARRIED IT FORWARD WITH NO INCONSIDERABLE SUCCESS.

In 1990, a News Service study reveals that US government intelligence compiled a list of names of Communist Party leaders and those of "mass organizations", mainly labour federations, women's and youth groups. The Americans furnished the Indonesian army with 5,000 names, checking off the names of those killed or captured. The CIA station chief refers to this as "a shooting list".

MANY PEOPLE HAD TO BE KEPT FOR INTERROGATION OR "KANGAROO COURTS" BECAUSE THE INDONESIANS DIDN'T HAVE ENOUGH GOON SQUADS TO ZAP THEM ALL.

Quotable quotes from two US State Department experts . . .

NO ONE CARED AS LONG AS THEY WERE COMMUNISTS THAT WERE BEING BUTCHERED.

THEY PROBABLY KILLED A LOT OF PEOPLE, AND I PROBABLY HAVE A LOT OF BLOOD ON MY HANDS, BUT THAT'S NOT ALL BAD.

The Nicaragua File

President **James Monroe** (1758–1831) issued his "doctrine" of 1823 which stated that any European interference in the New World would be regarded as a war-like act.

President **Theodore Roosevelt** (1858–1919) extended this "Monroe Doctrine" in 1904 to mean that the US felt free to interfere in a Latin American state guilty of "chronic wrong-doing".

The Monroe Doctrine has come to mean a policy of US domination in Latin America.

US Marines landed in Nicaragua in 1909 after a similar pattern of interventions in Cuba (1898), Honduras (1905) and Panama (1908). Nicaragua remained a US protectorate thereafter.

Augusto César Sandino (1893–1934), a pro-Liberal, began a successful guerrilla war in 1926 against the US Marines and their trained Nicaraguan National Guard.

The Sandinistas insisted on a redistribution of land to the peasantry, which was violently opposed by **Anastasio Somoza Garcia** (1896–1956), head of the National Guard.

Sandino was murdered by Somoza's National Guard in 1934. Somoza, a devoted US ally, seized control in 1937 and ran a brutal military dictatorship which remained in power under the Somoza dynasty until 1979, when it was finally overthrown by the Sandinista National Liberation Front, which enjoyed immense popular support.

President **Jimmy Carter** (b. 1924) tried desperately to prop up Somoza's régime to the bitter end. Israel was enlisted (despite US denials) in the final death agonies of a bloody régime. Nicaragua lay in ruins, the countryside devastated, with 40–50,000 killed.

When the Sandinistas are finally in government, everything is done to demonize them with accusations of genocide, drug-trafficking and undemocratic practices. The US media intellectuals keep silent about the documented facts of the Sandinistas' remarkable reforms.

From Oxfam's experience of working in 76 developing countries, Nicaragua's Sandinista government proved exceptional in its commitment to addressing inequities in land ownership, and in extending health, educational and agricultural services to poor peasant families.

Until 1989, the US pursues a policy of destabilization by supplying an insurgent army of "Contras" in Nicaragua.

The Rotten Apple Theory

The image given by the US as traditionally committed to the "defence of democracy" is a masterpiece of indoctrination. But the question is, why does the powerful US feel so threatened by socialism in smaller, weaker countries like Nicaragua, Chile and even tiny Grenada?

An explanation for this superficially quite irrational behaviour is provided by the rotten apple theory, in its internal rather than public form; in these terms, the hysteria makes perfect sense. If a tiny impoverished country with minuscule resources can begin to do something for its own population, others may ask: "Why not us?" The weaker and more insignificant a country, the more limited its means and resources, the greater the threat of a good example. The rot may spread, threatening regions of real concern to the rulers of much of the world.

Who's the Criminal?

One of Chomsky's methods of unmasking the tricks of indoctrination is by "the study of paired examples". Here are two examples of such pairings.

Compare cases **1** and **2**.

Case 1

A priest is murdered by policemen in communist Poland in 1984. The policemen are quickly apprehended, tried and jailed.

Result: massive, sustained outcry in the US media. Repetition of bloody details, allusions to Soviet involvement.

Case 2

100 prominent Latin American religious figures martyred, including the assassination of the Archbishop of San Salvador and four American churchwomen raped and murdered by the US-backed security forces.

Result: media restraint. Comments that a "basically moderate" government is finding it difficult to control violence of either the right or the left.

Case 1

Released Cuban prisoner Armando Valladares quickly becomes a media event. Invited by President Ronald Reagan to a White House ceremony on Human Rights Day in 1986.

Result: the media loudly condemns the bloody Cuban tyrant Fidel Castro, "yet another of this century's mass murderers" (*Washington Post*), and the "inhuman torture", the "bestial prisons" in Cuba.

Case 2

In 1986, director Herbert Anaya and almost the entire membership of CDHES, the non-governmental human rights commission of El Salvador, are arrested and tortured. They compile a 160-page report of sworn testimony from 430 political prisoners recording details of torture: in one case, by an American major in uniform.

Result: the report and a video testimony smuggled out of prison during the Valladares episode are almost completely suppressed by the American media. Anaya is eventually released and then assassinated.

Commissars and the Speciality Game

WHAT IS A COMMISSAR?

Commissars are those intellectuals who take part in social management in allegiance to state power and the exercise of it.

A prototypical example is the Soviet commissar. Another is the self-styled "action intellectual" of the Kennedy period. I do not find it terribly surprising that rule by these élites has led to extremes of state violence, arrogance and some of the ugliest episodes in American history.

A familiar ruse of the commissar is to attack the **competence** of someone's political analysis by saying something like . . .

The intellectual commissar does the opposite of Chomsky's "pairing of examples" by uncoupling the critic from the "specialist right" to speak, and thereby retaining power and thought control. There are media, academic and civil service commissars who form an intelligentsia or intellectual élite.

An indication of the real facts was given by an in-depth study of attitudes of "the American intellectual élite" undertaken in the spring of 1970, at the height of opposition to the Vietnam war after the US invasion of Cambodia, with universities shut down after student protests and popular dissidence reaching proportions that were quite frightening to élite groups. The results showed that virtually all were opposed to the war and would have been classified as doves. But when we turn to the reasons, we find that the overwhelming majority were opposed on "pragmatic grounds" – the war would not succeed in its aims – while a minority were opposed because the war was becoming too bloody (what the study called "moral grounds": a certain amount of killing, maiming and torture is legitimate, but too much may offend delicate souls). Principled opposition to the war was so negligible as to be barely detectable. Perhaps 1% of the intellectual sample opposed the war on the grounds that aggression is wrong, even if undertaken by the United States . . . In contrast, much of the *general population* opposed the war on grounds of principle. As late as the 1980s, after a decade of dedicated efforts to overcome the "Vietnam syndrome", over 70% of the population regarded the war as "fundamentally wrong and immoral", not merely a "mistake" as the official doves maintain.
Chomsky

There are no magic answers, no miraculous methods to overcome the problems we face, just the familiar ones: honest search for understanding, education, organization, action that raises the cost of state violence for its perpetrators or that lays the basis for institutional change – and the kind of commitment that will persist despite the temptations of disillusionment, despite many failures and only limited successes, inspired by the hope of a brighter future. Closing words of *Turning the Tide*

Bibliography

Works in Linguistics by Noam Chomsky

The Logical Structure of Linguistic Theory (Cambridge, MIT ms. 1955–6), Plenum, New York 1975
Syntactic Structures, Mouton, The Hague 1957
Review of B.F. Skinner's *Verbal Behavior*, **Language** 35, 35:26–58, 1959
Current Issues in Linguistic Theory, Mouton, The Hague 1964
Aspects of the Theory of Syntax, MIT Press, Cambridge, Mass. 1965
Cartesian Linguistics: a Chapter in the History of Rationalist Thought, Harper & Row, New York 1966
Topics in the Theory of Generative Grammar, Mouton, The Hague 1966
Language and Mind, Harcourt Brace Jovanovitch, New York 1968
Studies on Semantics in Generative Grammar, Mouton, The Hague 1972
Reflections on Language, Pantheon, New York 1975
Essays on Form and Interpretation, North-Holland, New York 1977
Morphophonemics of Modern Hebrew, Garland, New York 1979
Language and Responsibility, Pantheon, New York 1979
Rules and Representations, Columbia University Press, New York 1980
Lectures on Government and Binding: the Pisa Lectures, Foris, Cinnaminson 1982
Noam Chomsky on the Generative Enterprise: A Discussion with R. Huybregts and H. van Riemsdijk, Foris, Cinnaminson 1982
Some Concepts and Consequences of the Theory of Government and Binding, MIT Press, Cambridge, Mass. 1982
Modular Approaches to the Study of the Mind, California State University Press, San Diego 1984
Knowledge of Language: Its Nature, Origin and Use, Praeger, New York 1986
Barriers, MIT Press, Cambridge, Mass. 1986
Language in a Psychological Setting, Sophia Linguistica 22, Tokyo 1987
Language and the Problems of Knowledge: The Managua Lectures, MIT Press, Cambridge, Mass. 1988
Language and Thought, Moyer Bell, Wakefield, R.I. 1994
The Minimalist Program, MIT Press, Cambridge, Mass. 1995

Co-authored works

The Sound Pattern of English, N. Chomsky and M. Halle, Harper & Row, New York 1968

Political Writings

American Power and the New Mandarins, Pantheon, New York 1969

At War With Asia, Pantheon, New York 1970

Problems of Knowledge and Freedom: The Russell Lectures, Pantheon, New York 1971

For Reasons of State, Pantheon, New York 1973

Counter-Revolutionary Violence: Bloodbaths in Fact and Propaganda, Warner Modular, Andover, Mass. 1973 (with Edward Herman)

Peace in the Middle East? Reflections on Justice and Nationhood, Pantheon, New York 1974

"Human Rights" and American Foreign Policy, Spokesman, Nottingham, UK 1978

The Washington Connection and Third World Fascism, South End Press, Boston, Mass. 1979 (with Edward Herman)

Towards a New Cold War: Essays on the Current Crisis and How We Got There, Pantheon, New York 1982

The Fateful Triangle: The United States, Israel and the Palestinians, South End Press, Boston, Mass. 1983

The Culture of Terrorism, South End Press, Boston, Mass. 1988

Turning the Tide: US Intervention in Central America and the Struggle for Peace, South End Press, Boston, Mass. 1985

On Power and Ideology: The Managua Lectures, South End Press, Boston, Mass. 1987

Pirates and Emperors: International Terrorism in the Real World, Black Rose Books, Montreal 1987

Necessary Illusions: Thought Control in Democratic Societies, South End Press, Boston, Mass. 1989

Chronicles of Dissent, Common Courage Press, Monroe, Maine 1992

Deterring Democracy, Verso, New York 1992

Letters from Lexington: Reflections on Propaganda, Common Courage Press, Monroe, Maine 1992

What Uncle Sam Really Wants, Odonian Press, Tucson, Arizona 1992

Year 501: The Conquest Continues, South End Press, Boston, Mass. 1993

Keeping the Rabble in Line, Common Courage Press, Monroe, Maine 1994

Rethinking Camelot: JFK, the Vietnam War, and US Political Culture, South End Press, Boston, Mass. 1993

The Prosperous Few and the Restless Many, Odonian Press, Tucson, Arizona 1993

World Orders Old and New, Columbia University Press, New York 1994

Secrets, Lies and Democracy, Odonian Press, Tucson, Arizona 1994

Powers and Prospects: Reflections on Human Nature and the Social Order, South End Press, Boston, Mass. 1996

Co-authored works with Edward S. Herman

Counter-Revolutionary Violence: Bloodbaths in Fact and Propaganda,
Warner Modular, Andover, Mass. 1973
The Washington Connection and Third World Fascism, South End Press,
Boston, Mass. 1979
**After the Cataclysm: Postwar Indochina and the Reconstruction of
Imperial Ideology**, South End Press, Boston, Mass. 1979
Manufacturing Consent: the Political Economy of the Mass Media,
Pantheon, New York 1988

CD Recordings

The Clinton Vision: Old Wine, New Bottles, AK Press, Edinburgh 1993
Prospects for Democracy, AK Press, Edinburgh 1994
Class War: the Attack on Working People, AK Press, Edinburgh 1995

Collections

Chomsky: Selected Readings, J.P.B. Allen and P. van Buren, Oxford
University Press, Oxford 1971
Radical Priorities, C.P. Otero (ed.), Black Rose Books, Montreal 1984
The Chomsky Reader, J. Peck (ed.), Pantheon, New York 1987
Language and Politics, C.P. Otero (ed.), Black Rose Books, Montreal 1989

Books on Noam Chomsky

On Noam Chomsky: Critical Essays, Gilbert Harman (ed.), Anchor, New
York 1974
Chomsky's System of Ideas, Fred d'Agostino, Oxford University Press,
Oxford 1986
The Chomsky Update, Raphael Salkie, Unwin Hyman, London 1990
Chomsky, John Lyons, Fontana, London 1991 (3rd edition)
Noam Chomsky: Critical Assessments (volumes 1–4), Carlos P. Otero (ed.),
Routledge, London 1994
Manufacturing Consent: Noam Chomsky and the Media, Mark Achbar (ed.),
Black Rose Books, Montreal 1994
Chomsky's Universal Grammar: an Introduction, Vivian J. Cook and Mark
Newson, Blackwell, Oxford 1996
Chomsky's Politics, Milan Rai, Verso, London 1995

Films on Chomsky

Manufacturing Consent: Noam Chomsky and the Media, Peter Wintonick
and Mark Achbar, Canada 1982

Acknowledgements

Judy Groves and John Maher are indebted to Noam Chomsky for his patience and courtesy on the occasion of our visit to MIT, and for his encouragement and extensive comments on the final draft of the text. **Any mistakes or infelicities remain the responsibility of the author and artist.**

John Maher thanks colleagues for their encouragement or advice during the writing of this book, in particular Ron Asher, George Bedell, Roger Buckley, Alan Davies, Bates Hoffer, Shaun Malarney, Aya Nishizono-Maher and Suzanne Quay. My thanks go to Richard Appignanesi for his intelligent work on the manuscript and for his encouraging faxes which kept my engine firing; to Peter Pugh for calmly keeping the faith in the project and the saké warm, on a Tokyo winter's night; to Duncan Heath for his cool professionalism in the face of critical deadlines and summer heat; to the unemployed man on a bus from Harvard Square to MIT for his erudition on poverty and wealth in Boston and his encouragement to do this book with his words: "When I first heard Chomsky speak, I just wanted to run out into the street and shout: 'Hey listen, listen! Somebody's telling the truth!'"

Judy Groves thanks Oscar Zarate for the illustrations on pages 12, 72, 73, 84, 102, 116, 129, 138 and 164; Colin Smith for technical assistance; and David King for his help with picture research.

About the authors

John Maher studied philosophy and linguistics in London, Michigan and Edinburgh. He has published ten books on: bilingualism, Ainu, language rights, and the languages of Japan. He lives and works in Tokyo where he is Professor of Linguistics at International Christian University. John dedicates this book to his daughter Sophie, to whom he offers Chomsky's comment: "If you assume that there is an instinct for freedom, there are opportunities to change things. There's a chance you may contribute to making a better world."

Judy Groves is an artist, illustrator and designer. She has also illustrated introductory guides to Jesus, Lacan, Wittgenstein, Lévi-Strauss and Philosophy.

Handlettering by **Woodrow Phoenix**
Typesetting by **Wayzgoose**

Index